I love the US West Coast
travel guide

By S. L. Giger as *SwissMiss on Tour*

"Oh, the places you'll go!"
— Dr. Seuss.

Copyright © 2022 Seraina Cavalli-Giger
www.swissmissontour.com
All rights reserved.
ISBN: 9798353063308

The work including its parts is protected by copyright. Any use outside the limits of copyright law is prohibited without the written consent of the publisher and the author.
This applies in particular to electronic or other duplication, translation, distribution, and public disclosure.
The advice in this book has been carefully considered and verified by the author. However, all information in this book is provided without any warranty or guarantee on the part of the publisher or the author. Any liability of the author or the publisher and its agents for personal injury, property damage or financial loss is also excluded.
Self-published. Contact: Seraina Cavalli:
swissmissontour@gmail.com
Cover design: Seraina Cavalli
Cover pictures: Christoph Partscha from Pixabay (Golden Gate Bridge) and KeYang from Pixabay (Horseshoe Bend)
First Edition
Printed by Amazon

Receive a free packing list

Never forget anything important ever again and don't waste unnecessary time with packing. Scan the QR code and receive a free packing list along with a sample of my Thailand travel guide.

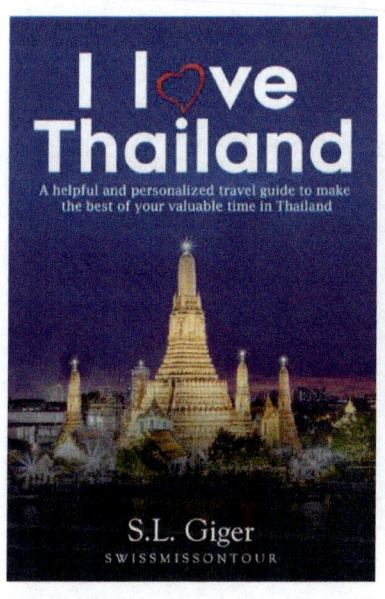

Content

I love the US West Coast..1

Receive a free packing list...3

Why should I choose this guidebook instead of any other?..........7

Reasons to look forward to your journey......................................9

USA West Coast Highlights 10

Things to consider before you visit the US 12

    Visa, Vaccinations, and other entry requirements 12

    Covid requirements 13

    Currency...14

    Drinking water 15

    When is the best time to visit the US? 16

    Renting a car in the US...17

    Driving distances and times...20

    Public transport in the US 22

    How to find a travel buddy 23

    Finding your way..25

    Typical American food and drinks 26

    How to pick your accommodation...29

    Wi-Fi...30

    Tips on how to find cheap flights to the US.............................31

Three-week itinerary to see the best of the Western USA..........34

Las Vegas, Nevada 41

How to get from the airport to the strip 41

What to do in Las Vegas 42

Route 66 47

Visiting the National Parks along the West Coast of the USA 48

Grand Canyon 49

Page, Arizona 52

Horseshoe Bend 52

Lake Powell 53

Antelope Canyon 54

Monument Valley 56

Arches National Park 57

Grand Staircase-Escalante National Monument 60

Bryce Canyon 62

Zion National Park 64

Death Valley 66

San Diego 69

How to get from the airport to the city center 69

The best things to do in San Diego 69

Los Angeles 73

How to get from the airport to the city center 74

The best things to do in L.A. 74

Highway #1 80

Santa Barbara, Solvang, and Pismo Beach 81

Morro Bay, Big Sur, Monterrey, Santa Cruz 82

- Half Moon Bay – San Francisco 85
- San Francisco 86
  - How to get from the airport to the city center 86
  - The best things to do in San Francisco 87
- Yosemite National Park 91
  - The top things to do at Yosemite 92
- Red Wood drive-through trees and distance to Seattle 94
- Portland 95
  - From the airport to the city center 95
- Seattle 97
  - From the airport to the city center 97
  - The best things to do in Seattle 98
- Border Crossing into Canada: Seattle to Vancouver 101
- About the author of this guidebook 102
- Do you need more info? 103
- Did you like this travel guide? 103
- More books by S. L. Giger 104

Why should I choose this guidebook instead of any other?

Do you only have a limited amount of time to travel (like two or three weeks) and feel a bit overwhelmed about which places you should visit? Should you spend more time in famous coastal cities like San Francisco or Los Angeles or hike or drive in the beautiful national parks of the Western USA? The West Coast of the USA offers a wide variety of stunning places. It might be difficult to choose and settle on a route. This guidebook will help you to focus on the must-sees of California, Nevada, Arizona, Utah, and Seattle in Washington. Marvel at enchanted landscapes, take the most beautiful road trips the USA has to offer, jump into the Pacific Ocean, or watch sea lions go about their business. Feel like a star in Hollywood, eat delicious Mexican food in San Diego, cross the Golden Gate Bridge and visit the best museums or a fun theme park. *I love USA West Coast* will guide you on how to do that and much more.

With *I love USA West Coast*, you won't have to do any further research. You find a three-week travel itinerary with detailed "how-to"-guidelines and further ideas and descriptions.

Do you want to plan your own, smooth journey in California and visit the best national parks along the West Coast? This guidebook will help you to do just that.

I have visited the West Coast on several trips. First, on a road trip with my family to see the Southwest. Later, we returned to see more of the Northwest, always with a stop in California, to visit the family we have there. A road trip with a car is definitely the most convenient way to travel in the US (or by motorbike if that is your thing). However, it also is possible if you don't want to drive or can't drive. On one of my trips, I returned as a solo backpacker and also had a really fun time. It's easy to travel by bus or train between the big cities. However, to re-visit the national parks in the Southwest (because they are simply too beautiful not to visit, once you are so close by) I teamed up with another solo traveler and we rented a car together. Therefore, I will include tips on how to rent a car in the US, as well as how to travel by public transport, and how to find a travel companion.

Doing a road trip on your own can be incredibly peaceful as you have all of nature to yourself and can enjoy it as long or short as you like. Normally, I encourage going on solo trips as it's no problem to meet other travelers along the way in case you start feeling lonely. Yet, in the US it was a bit more difficult since most people already traveled in pre-arranged groups and pretty much stay in their cars. Hence, at least for visiting the national parks, I would recommend that you find people to share this amazing experience with and create wonderful memories together.

Every day, you will experience a new highlight and I am sure that you'll enjoy your trip to the USA as much as I did.

Woohoo, time to start planning, enjoy your adventure in the Western USA!

Reasons to look forward to your journey along the amazing US West Coast

Probably, this chapter is a bit superfluous in this travel guide as the US West Coast and the national parks attract millions of visitors each year. That doesn't mean that you should skip it because everyone has been there already anyway.

The bustling cities are still rich in art, culture, and modern architecture. Las Vegas will impress you with the vast variety of hotels and restaurants even if you don't spend a cent on gambling. Beaches invite you to live the California dream or head into the waves for a surf. Last but not least the national parks like Grand Canyon or Bryce Canyon are so beautiful and vast that you will feel like a small person, thankful to be able to visit such stunning places on our planet.

So, it's pretty likely that you will also fall in love with the many wonders the US West Coast has to offer, and after going there once, you might already be dreaming about when to go back next.

USA West Coast Highlights

The Western USA certainly has a highlight for everyone. Whether you prefer chic restaurants where you can people-watch in your summer dress, theme parks with thrilling rides, or nature that makes you wonder how it got created, you will find many treasures. Hence, it's hard to name only three highlights and they are entirely subjective to my taste. But here are my three favorites along the US West Coast.

1 Bryce Canyon

This canyon in Utah looks like a giant has played with wet sand and has built dripping sandcastles. Afterward, he dusted the creations with different hues of white and orange. The whole landscape looks magical and it's an incredible place to take a walk.

2 San Diego

San Diego is the city I would choose to live in the US. The weather is great, and you have nice beaches for surfing, bathing, or snorkeling. Further, the downtown area is pretty and offers entertaining nightlife. Plus, you will find so many good places to eat that it's hard not to be disappointed by the food in other cities afterward.

3 Big Sur

Big Sur is an area along Highway 1 in California. I take it as a representative of this incredibly beautiful drive along the West coast. You get to see stunning cliffs and natural bays where sea animals can find a resting place before going out fishing again. If you ever wanted to take a road trip, Highway One should be at the top of your list.

Things to consider before you visit the US to have the best possible trip

In case you are from the US and currently reading this guide, most of the following information probably won't interest you since you already know how everything works. However, as a tourist coming to the US, you might have heard from other people or experienced on past trips that there is quite a lot you need to consider, in order to even be allowed to enter the country. With COVID, there are even more rules in place. But don't worry, and don't let that stop you from traveling to the US. I was fifteen the first time I came to the US – alone as part of an exchange year. I didn't speak much English then and the questions they asked at the customs control were a bit intimidating. However, in the end, it was an easy step-by-step process. You should have no problems with starting your trip when you read the following information.

Visa, Vaccinations, and other entry requirements

If you want to stay in the US for up to 90 days, you need a biometric passport. You don't need to apply for a visa if your country is part of the ESTA visa waiver program. You can check on this website if your country is part of the ESTA agreement: www.dhs.gov/visa-waiver-program-requirements
Then, you have to fill in the ESTA form up to 72h before you start your trip on this website: https://esta.cbp.dhs.gov/esta
Don't be late with this online application! You will have to enter your personal details and travel details. If everything is filled in correctly, you might be able to pass through an electronic gate once you arrive at a US airport without having to answer any further questions about your trip. If any information is missing or if they are double-checking, they will ask you about the purpose of your visit, how long, and where you are planning to stay.

Perhaps, you will also have to leave your fingerprints on a digital field.

The validation of the ESTA costs $14 and your ESTA status then will be active for 2 years. You can use it for multiple trips. If the website asks for more than $14 you are likely not on the official page of the US government.

Vaccinations

The CDC recommends the common routine vaccinations for everyone.
If you are staying longer than 90 days you will have to apply for a different visa and probably, it will be mandatory to complete all the required routine vaccinations for the US.

Covid requirements

- At the time of writing this book, non-US-citizens that are 18 or older are required to be fully vaccinated against COVID-19. This means you need to have completed your vaccination doses with an officially accepted vaccine at least two weeks before traveling to the US (no booster). This also applies to recovered people.
- In addition, people of 2 years and older have to present a negative antigen or PCR test which is less than 24 h old.

If you fail to present a proof of vaccination or a test at the airport, you won't be allowed to board the plane.

Since COVID requirements could change very quickly, here are some general rules of what you have to check before traveling during times of COVID.

1. What regulations does the USA currently have? Can your nationality enter the country? Do you need proof of a test or a vaccine?

2. Are there any obligations when returning to your country?
You might need to get an antigen test or a PCR test and perhaps the US is on your country's quarantine list.

3. Do you need a test or vaccine for the airline you are flying with or because of the stopover you are having?
Best contact the airline for information about that if you aren't sure.

Currency

Of course, you know that the US uses the green US dollar. The short form is USD and the symbol $. At the moment of writing this book, 1 GBP equaled 1.23 USD and 1 AUD was 70 US cents. 1 Canadian dollar equaled 0.77 USD. To have the correct conversion during your trip, use Google and search for USD to GBP (or the currency that you use).

In the US you can pay with a credit card or a debit card pretty much everywhere and you find ATMs at gas stations, banks, and inside bigger shops.
In case your ATM card has an international surcharge fee it's best to withdraw as much money as you will need for your trip at once. Of course, you can also exchange money at the airport, but they will probably give you a bad exchange rate.

For security reasons, don't keep the whole wad of cash in your wallet but divert it to a few places on your luggage. Only take as much money outside of the accommodation as you need for the time being.

Be aware that there is a sales tax on most things that you buy. The tax varies between the states but on average, it's 5 %. So, if you purchase a souvenir magnet for $1 you will actually have to pay $1.05.

Drinking water

The tap water in the US should be drinkable since the Clean Water Act of 1972. However, recent investigations have shown elevated levels of toxic ingredients in many locations across the US. Therefore, I recommend bringing a travel water filter. You can buy them online or in outdoor stores or travel shops. This way, you can still drink tap water and in addition, won't produce plastic waste by buying 1.5 to 3 liters of water every day.
Often, hotels or motels have a free water dispenser with filtered water where you could refill your bottle.
In restaurants, you usually receive free tap water. I always drink that tap water and never had any problems with my stomach.

When is the best time to visit the US?

You will have an enjoyable time in the US all year round. If you want to swim in the ocean or are hoping for a lot of sunshine and warm weather, you have to travel between July and September.

While October is not so warm anymore, it's still a good month to travel, especially if you visit places with many trees. Forests will be colored in intense hues of orange, yellow, and red and it might be fun to visit a pumpkin farm or participate in Halloween events.

Winter is mild in California with temperatures between 12 and 20 degrees Celsius for coastal regions. While in Seattle it can go down to around 4 degrees. With the opulent Christmas decorations in the big cities, December also is a nice month to visit the US, if you didn't want to spend too much time at the beach.
On the other hand, the mountain ranges also receive a lot of snow. Especially in the area of Yosemite National Park you often are required to put snow chains on the tires of your car. Plus, the North Rim of the Grand Canyon is closed from December to 15 May. The South Rim is open all year and so that's no problem for our highlight travel itinerary.

Spring is beautiful since it gets even sunnier and warmer, plus, the landscape looks greener or there are more flowers than usual. However, the schools' spring breaks take place between mid-March through mid-April, and then the top travel destinations are crowded with partying school kids. Hence, you might want to avoid traveling during those weeks.

Throughout the entire year, it's a good idea to bring along a softshell jacket since there can be a breeze in coastal cities. Especially in San Francisco, I have already been freezing on foggy days in August. But you wanted to buy a cuddly "I love San Francisco" sweater anyway, right :D?

Renting a car in the US

You are probably aware that the US is a country made for cars. There are long, straight roads leading through incredible landscapes on which you can cover big distances. Multi-lane highways connect cities so that it might seem scary at first to even enter the highway. But don't worry, just go with the flow, and pay good attention before changing lanes. Then, you will be fine.

Traveling by car will make your life easier, especially if you want to visit the national parks. You have the freedom to leave and arrive whenever you please. Plus, there usually are plenty of (free) parking spots available everywhere (except in the very downtown areas of major cities). Further, I am sure you want to experience a true American road trip as you know it from the movies. So, book your rental car, grab some road trip snacks and an iced coffee, and start your self-drive trip.

Requirements for renting a car in the US

As a tourist, you need
- to be 21 years (18 for New York and Michigan) or older
- to have a valid driver's license
- an international driver's license if your license is not in English
- to pay extra insurance if you are younger than 25 and perhaps, they won't let you rent the biggest size of cars
- a passport or ID
- a credit card

The rental companies

There are many rental companies, and you should check for the best deal online before you arrive in the US. It's best to reserve your preferred rental car in advance because then, you only have to fill in a small amount of paperwork once you arrive at the pick-up point at the airport (or in town, in case you don't need the car right away). In addition, it might be hard to find a suitable rental car last minute during busy tourist seasons. Hence, it's better to plan ahead.

Even with this preparation, it usually took us up to 1.5 hours until we had the car because the rental places were always so busy. Therefore, calculate some time for the pickup.
When everything is ok with the car, the drop-off usually is much faster and smoother since you simply drive into the assigned garage or parking lot and drop off the keys.

Which car should you choose?

For economic and ecological reasons, I would recommend that you travel in a small car like a VW beetle if you are only two people. The car was perfectly reliable on all the roads we traveled in the national

parks or along the coast. However, I understand if you are dreaming of a big car with lots of space and big wheels. It certainly is very American, and, in most places, you won't have any trouble finding a parking space even for a big car.
Make sure that you book an automatic car in case you don't like to drive stick shifts.

Safety tips for renting a car

With so many people using the roads, accidents occur daily. The problem often occurs in cities or on highways when people talk or text on the phone while driving. You will shake your head at how many people you will see on the phone in their car, although we all know how dangerous that is. Therefore, just like with skiing, be sure to think for yourself as well as the other drivers while you are behind the wheel and be extra alert.

Another danger is people who are speeding or running red lights.

It's more relaxed to drive on rural roads or inside the national parks. There, the only danger is that you are distracted by the beauty of the landscape and swerve off the road. Therefore, better frequently stop at the available viewing platforms and take in the surroundings then (not while you are sitting behind the wheel).

One more danger is theft if anything of value is visible in the car. Better don't leave anything visible in the car when you are not in it or are driving with the windows down. Plus, always lock it, when you get out of your car, even if you think that you only step out for 2 minutes to enjoy the view.

Driving distances and times

Here is a chart with the distances and times for the routes you might be driving. In case you travel by public transport, check the times on the websites in the next chapter.

The Southwestern National Parks and Las Vegas

Start	Destination	Distance	Time
Los Angeles	Las Vegas	270 mi/ 435 km	4h 15 mins
San Diego	Las Vegas	332 mi/ 535 km	5h 15 mins
Las Vegas	Grand Canyon South Rim	280 mi/ 450 km	4h 25 mins
Grand Canyon South Rim	Page	130 mi/ 210 km	2h 25 mins
Page	Monument Val.	126 mi/ 202 km	2h 20 mins
Monument Valley	Moab	150 mi/ 240 km	2h 35 mins
Moab	Escalante	220 mi/ 355 km	4h
Escalante	Bryce Canyon	50 mi / 80 km	1h
Bryce Canyon	Zion NP	85 mi / 137 km	2h
Zion NP	Las Vegas	160 mi/ 260 km	2h 40 mins
Las Vegas	Death Valley	130 mi/ 210 km	2h 20 mins
Death Valley	San Diego	360 mi/ 580 km	6h

The West Coast

Here are the most frequent distances that tourists cover along Highway 1 or Highway 101.

San Diego	Los Angeles	125 mi/ 200 km	2h
Los Angeles	Malibu	33 mi / 53 km	35 mins
Los Angeles	Santa Barbara	100 mi/ 160 km	2h
Santa Barbara	Pismo Beach	90 mi / 145 km	1h 40 mins
Pismo Beach	Santa Cruz	190 mi/ 305 km	4h
Monterrey	San Francisco	120 mi/ 193 km	2h
San Francisco	Yosemite	200 mi/ 320 km	3h 45 mins
Yosemite	Sacramento	165 mi/ 265 km	3h 25 mins
Sacramento	Eureka	290 mi/ 467 km	5h 10 mins
Eureka	Portland	410 mi/ 660 km	7h 30 mins
Portland	Seattle	175 mi/ 282 km	2h 50 mins
Seattle	Vancouver, CA	145 mi/ 233 km	2h 30 mins

Public transport in the US

Frequent traffic jams in city centers have led to good public transport systems in all major cities. While bus routes can still seem slow or chaotic, if you have the option to travel by metro or tram, you will most likely be quicker than by car. You can check your best public transport connection within a city on google maps.

Traveling between cities

Traveling between the bigger cities is no problem anymore. There are many comfortable coach buses or even trains to choose from. The travel time is a bit slower than if you travel by car since you stop at several bus stations along the way and you have to adhere to the schedules on when the buses or trains are leaving. On the upside, you can look out the window while being on a bus or train and don't have to be concentrated as if you were driving. Enjoy the landscape you pass by, read a book, or start writing your travel diary. Traveling by public transport can definitely be a relaxing way of relocation.

In order to buy a ticket or check the available routes and times, you can compare the following websites:
- www.rome2rio.com/de/map/San-Francisco/Seattle
- https://shop.flixbus.com/
- www.omio.com/

For example, a bus trip between LA and San Diego takes about 2h 40mins and costs around $11. The quickest connection between LA and Las Vegas would take 5h 10mins and costs around $24.

Along the coast, there is also a **train line** available, which is operated by Amtrak: www.amtrak.com/tickets/departure.html

When I was backpacking in the US, I actually took the train trip between San Francisco and Seattle, which took 24 h. Somehow, I had a romantic idealization of spending the night on the train and having lots of time to read and look out of the window. While many passages were pretty, in the end, it was simply too long (because on top, we had a delay), and I wouldn't do it again. Perhaps, it's better to check inland flights, in case you want to cover bigger distances.

Public transport to discover the national parks

Unfortunately, there is no public transport with which you could conveniently visit the national parks in the Western USA.

You are left with two options: team up with someone to rent a car or join a day tour. Las Vegas is a good base for organized day tours to Grand Canyon, Zion, or Bryce Canyon and hence you have no excuse not to go there, even if you don't have a driver's license. Plus, you will probably meet nice fellow travelers on your tour and perhaps you even decide to do another tour together.

How to find a travel buddy

After university, I embarked on a trip around the world – solo. None of my friends had so much time off or wanted to take the same route but starting the trip alone didn't matter. One thing I've learned over the years is that there are always other open-minded travelers who want to talk to you or spend time with you.

In Southeast Asia, it was never necessary to worry about companionship since there are so many other solo travelers following the exact same backpacker trail. So, you are actually glad when you have some time to yourself and surely won't have to previously look for a travel buddy online.

In Australia, the most convenient way to travel was by car and therefore, I looked for people to do road trips with. It was easy because Australia has an online marketplace called *gumtree*, on which you can find anything from electric toothbrushes to travel partners. This in a short amount of time.

In the US, there was no gumtree marketplace for travel buddies. On top of that, it seemed that most travelers arrived in pre-arranged groups of friends or as families. There was a blackboard at my hostel in Las Vegas where you could look for a travel mate but unfortunately, nobody else was looking for someone. And I really didn't want to take a road trip on my own. Plus, renting a car at younger than 25 would have been very expensive. That left me with **Facebook travel buddy groups** and **Couchsurfing** (www.couchsurfing.org).

It certainly would have been easier to plan beforehand. To find a travel buddy online while still being at home and setting a date when we'd meet somewhere in the US to start our trip. That would have given me more time. But since I had been traveling for 9 months, I hadn't planned this part ahead and it was a bit frustrating to be in Las Vegas and hope that someone else would be looking online to do a national park tour with a travel buddy. After two days, I found someone and after some cheap margaritas at one of the casinos, we knew we had a similar idea of what our tour should look like. Since we got along well, we planned the tour and reserved the rental car. It turned out to be a great time and we even continued to San Francisco together afterward.

So, you see, it's possible to find travel buddies on social media or travel platforms and have a great trip. However, you might have to be a bit spontaneous and also quite open-minded. Otherwise, you will feel more comfortable on organized group tours.

Finding your way

As everywhere I go, I used the **maps.me** app on my phone and downloaded the states I was visiting for offline use. This has been an extremely useful companion every day and always brought me to the place I wanted to go. You can use maps.me to find points of interest within a city, to get to your accommodation, or to follow a hiking route (for example in Zion National Park). Tourists can mark spots and write comments and hence you can even discover secret spots which other tourists recommend.

Typical American food and drinks

The US is known for many mouthwatering delicacies, whether it is a perfect steak, juicy burger, or donuts. If you only nourish yourself with those dishes, you will certainly gain weight and probably have a heart attack soon. However, you are on vacation, right? Therefore, perhaps ignore the calories or sugar level for once and try the following US dishes during your visit to the USA.

- **Hamburger with French Fries**

Americans have perfected the hamburgers. You can find them with any topping you wish and delicious sauces. Therefore, you should not limit your road trip to McDonald's visits but also try burgers in different restaurants along the way. Fries might come thin and crispy, or like thick cuts, curly or as potato wedges. Hence, it won't get boring.

- **Bagels**

Bagels are circular-shaped pieces of bread with a hole in the center. Pretty much a donut out of bread dough. The most common one is a bagel filled with cream cheese. It's delicious for breakfast as well as for a picnic lunch. But you can also fill it with any topping you love, be it salmon or arugula. Come to think of it, a true American bagel is the American food I miss most.

- **Donuts and milkshakes**

Nowhere in the world do donuts taste as good as they do in the US. You can pick between different chain shops or find treasures in local bakeries. Eat your way through the different flavors to find your favorite one. Of course, it's great to wash it down with a sweet, flavored coffee or with an even sweeter milkshake. Who doesn't love a good Oreo shake?

- **Steak, BBQ ribs, or chicken wings**

Especially the Southern states are known for their good BBQs. However, you can find great steaks, flavorful spareribs, or well-marinated chicken wings in pretty much any steakhouse along the road. That being said, we know by now that eating meat is worse for the environment than flying or driving a car. Hence, you might want to make those meals count and only treat yourself to a really good piece of meat once or twice during your trip.

- **Lobster or scallops**

In the movies, it's often the rich who enjoy lobster in expensive restaurants. In Europe, this image is perfected because lobster is a very expensive type of seafood and so are the tender, round scallops. The good news is that you can eat lobster in the US for much cheaper. There even is a restaurant chain, called *Red Lobster*, where you can afford to eat with your whole family. So, if you ever wondered what lobster actually tastes like, here is your chance.

- **Tacos**

Tacos are probably Mexico's national dish and therefore, not typical American. However, the closer you get to Mexico, the more you will encounter Mexican restaurants and food trucks. So, in many towns in southern California, you will be able to eat absolutely authentic and delicious Mexican tacos. Either they consist of hard corn shells that are filled with toppings like meat, lettuce, cilantro, and lime plus a tasty sauce, or the tortilla is made of soft wheat.

Apart from great Mexican food, you can also find incredibly delicious Chinese food in the US. Try the sweet and sour chicken or dim sum dumplings and you will want to return to the US just for eating Chinese or Mexican food.

- **Hot Dog or Corn Dog**

In the US, a hot dog isn't simply a boring sausage on a slice of soft bread, but you can fill it with gherkins, fried onions, marinated onions, and other salsas. Hence it might even turn out to be a high-quality culinary experience. And this from a simple street food cart.

A corn dog is a German sausage that is placed on a stick, wrapped in corn dough, and then deep-fried. You can often find it at beach piers, summer fairs, and festivals. You can dip it into mustard or various other sauces.

- **Peanut butter and jelly sandwich**

If you aren't allergic to peanuts, this is the American breakfast food you really have to try as it's simply so famous. A PB&J sandwich is made by spreading a layer of peanut butter on a slice of bread and then covering the peanut butter layer with a fruity marmalade. Then, you top it with another slice of bread. It's the perfect combination of sweet and salty.
(After writing this, I have to run to the store and buy some peanut butter in order to satisfy my craving.)

Tipping in the USA

Waiters in the US have an extremely low minimum income. It's pre-calculated that a big part of their salary is made out of tips by the customers. That's why Americans are usually very generous when they travel abroad. So, don't be stingy when you come to the US. It's customary to tip 15 to 20 percent of the amount on your bill before taxes. This applies to sit-down restaurants, bars, and cafés. If you just pick up takeaway or buy food from a street-food cart, you don't have to leave a tip.

How to pick your accommodation

Since travelers all have their individual preferences about what standard their accommodation needs to be, I hardly include recommendations for hostels or hotels. Average travelers in the US mostly stay at motel chains like *Super 8*, *Motel 6*, or *Best Western* hotels. Check their reviews on **booking.com** and compare the prices with the website of the hotel. If you want more local experiences, you should look for gems on **Airbnb**.
During local holidays and other special occasions, you should pre-book.

In the US you will also come across many charming campgrounds where you can rent cabins or sleep in your tent. Perhaps, that's something you want to bring along in order to save some money or be closer to nature.

Wi-Fi

All of our accommodations offered free Wi-Fi. Further, there is free Wi-Fi at Starbucks, McDonald's, and most restaurants. Hence, you don't necessarily need to have personal data. If you think you want to make phone calls or need unlimited data anyway, better check with your phone provider at home how much a tourist addition for the US would be for the duration of your trip. For me, it would have been cheaper to top up my plan at home than to purchase a tourist sim card in the US.

Tips on how to find cheap flights to the US (and to any other country for that matter)

Sometimes, you can find real bargains from Europe to New York or Las Vegas. So cheap in fact, that you might even consider flying across the ocean for a weekend. However, think about the environment and better go when you have more time to stay there. The other cities in the US normally aren't that cheap to fly into but you can find good deals if you look for your ticket with the following strategy.

1. Use several flight search engines

I usually start looking for flights on **Skyscanner** and then I compare the deals from there with **CheapTickets** and/or **Opodo**. These sites tend to have the cheapest prices. Skyscanner for example, lets you set a price alert which will inform you with an e-mail when they have cheaper flights. You could do that half a year before your trip. Another possibility is to type your flight into Google directly to get an estimate of how much the airfare will be. In the end, I always check the websites of my favorite airlines directly. For the US, they are Swiss and KLM.

2. Be early and buy your flight at least 3 months in advance

If you know the dates of your vacation, there is no use to wait with booking your flights. They will only get more expensive. However, if you are very flexible with your plans, check last-minute deal sites like Urlaubsguru.de for cheap last-minute seats.

On the other hand: In times of covid, you should plan all your travel last-minute. Once you are sure that the country you want to visit is open and it will be agreeable to travel under the current circumstances.

3. Be slightly flexible

Check the dates three days prior to and after the dates, you chose to fly. There might be a difference of up to $300! If you search with CheapTickets or Skyscanner it's very easy to have an overview of the flight prices on different dates.

4. Travel from other airports and book multi-leg flights

Especially if you travel from Europe, it makes sense to check the airports in the surrounding countries and then buy a connecting flight from your country to get there (or better a train ride). Cheaper airports to fly from are Amsterdam, London, Frankfurt am Main, Munich, Paris, and Milan. So, yes, if you have enough time, it's sometimes worth it to travel in several legs. If you fly to the US, often Miami and New York are the cheapest on the East Coast while LAX and Las Vegas are the cheapest on the West Coast. Just calculate enough time in your connecting airport in case your first plane is delayed because you will have to get your luggage and check it in for your new flight.
With our sample itinerary, you will have to book a multi-leg flight, flying to Las Vegas and returning from Seattle.

Bear in mind: In times of covid, you should opt for a direct flight, since every additional stop can mean more tests, more regulations, and possible quarantine.

5. Delete your browser history

The websites where you searched for your flight tickets to the US will recognize you on your second visit and raise the prices a little since you are still interested. So, if you notice an increase in the price, the first thing to do is to close the website, clear the browser history and then start searching again once you are ready to book. It's astounding, how quickly you can save money this way.

6. Sign up for the newsletter from your favorite airlines

Newsletters still offer substantial value and often you find cheap airfares in them. At the moment, I regularly receive exclusive offers from TUI and KLM. By the way, SwissMissOnTour.com offers a newsletter as well. Sign up on the website to receive my latest blog posts and a free and helpful packing list.

Three-week itinerary to see the best of culture and nature in the Western USA

With an area this vast, it's difficult to cover so many highlights, simply because you also need time for driving from A to B. However, in the Western USA, the trip itself can also be counted as a highlight and with the following itinerary you won't miss out on anything. Have fun exploring all of these natural wonders and famous cities.

Day 1: Las Vegas

Once you arrive in this bustling city, it's time to shake your muscles from the flight and get ready to explore the hotel designs along the strip. Perhaps you want to gamble while enjoying cheap but good cocktails or maybe you're more interested in the shopping opportunities and food options. However, don't go to bed too late since you want to have energy for the start of your road trip tomorrow.

Day 2: Las Vegas to Grand Canyon South Rim

Pick up your rental car if you haven't done so yesterday and drive the 4 hours to the South Rim Visitor Center of the Grand Canyon. Along the way, you can make a short detour to look at the **Hoover Dam** and leave the highway to drive part of the iconic **Route 66**.
Buy the annual *America the Beautiful National Park Pass* at the entry gate. Check out the viewpoints in the park and do a leisurely hike along the rim or even rent a bicycle.
Stay in the national park as long as you please and then either choose a place to spend the night in this area or already head toward Page in Arizona.

Day 3: Antelope Canyon Horseshoe Bend and Lake Powell

If you spent the night at Grand Canyon, get up in time to cover the 2.5 hours to Page, in order to make it to your tour of the Antelope Canyon (which you pre-booked online). Before or after your tour you can head to Lake Powell and perhaps even take a dip in the lake. At the latest before sunset, you need to make it to the incredible Horseshoe Bend lookout and enjoy this special view of the Colorado River.

Day 4: Monument Valley to Moab and Arches National Park

Maybe your first thought today is that you have to check out the view at Horseshoe Bend again. After you have satisfied that need, you drive to Monument Valley. Join a jeep tour through Monument Valley or drive the bumpy loop in your rental car.

Afterward, continue another 2.5 hours to Moab. This is a very scenic drive on its own and in case you want to have more time in Arches National Park, feel free to skip entering the Monument Valley visitor's area entirely.

Inside Arches National Park you can opt for the shorter hikes that still lead you to the most amazing rock structures.

Day 5: Bryce Canyon

On your drive to Bryce Canyon, you can enjoy another extremely scenic drive on Bypass 12 toward Escalante. You could stop for one of the hikes near Escalante or drive to the enchanted Bryce Canyon directly. Here it's worth doing a hike that descends to the valley, where you are completely surrounded by the hoodoos.

Spend the night near Bryce Canyon.

Day 6: Zion National Park and Las Vegas

Drive to Zion NP and with that, reach a greener valley than the red desert you have seen during the past days. Take a hike or two in this beautiful place. Then, continue to Las Vegas, where you can spend more time at the casinos or visit a shopping outlet.

Day 7: Death Valley to San Diego

Today lies a long driving day ahead of you since the complete trip to Las Vegas via Death Valley would take about 8 hours. With stops in Death Valley, you can make it 12 hours. Hence, perhaps you won't make it all the way to San Diego today but just pick a motel along the way. The most important is that you marvel at the curious views inside Death Valley and take time for stops at roadside cafés.

Day 8: San Diego

Today, you could even leave the car in your hotel's parking lot and travel by public transport instead. Visit Balboa Park and the beaches of La Jolla. Congratulations, you have arrived at the Pacific Ocean! Either you will be greeted by surfers or sea lions or even both. Spend the evening in the Gaslamp Quarter.

Add a day here if you can and visit San Diego Zoo, more beaches, and the old town.

Day 9: Los Angeles with Santa Monica

Drive to L. A. and check out a museum downtown or just look at the architectural highlights from the outside. Then, head to Venice Beach but be sure to also stroll along the pier of Santa Monica.

Day 10: Hollywood

Today is all about the most famous locations in this movie-centered part of town. Read the stars on the Walk of Fame, take pictures of the famous theaters, and of course of the Hollywood sign. Then, go people-watch along Rodeo Drive. Either take a tour of the homes of the stars in Beverly Hills or do something more culturally enriching and visit the Getty Museum or Getty Villa.

Day 11: Disneyland or Universal Studios

There are lots of fun theme parks surrounding L. A. If you are old school or a Disney fan, you should visit the first Disneyland in Anaheim. In case you prefer more modern rides along with a great behind-the-scenes movie tour, spend the day at Universal Studios.

Day 12: Begin your road trip along Highway 1

Start your day early. You've probably already felt itchy feet in the past days because you've hardly done any driving. Today, you continue your road trip by starting one of the most picturesque drives on earth. The part between Santa Monica and Malibu is especially lovely.
Stop in Santa Barbara to enjoy a few hours of beach life and then continue to Solvang and Pismo Beach.

Day 13: Picturesque bays and wildlife along the coast

It's another day filled with highlights along the Pacific Coast Highway. Must-do stops are in Morro Bay, Big Sur, and Monterrey. Decide along the way whether you want to spend the night in Monterrey or already drive to Santa Cruz where you have a lively pier area.

Day 14: San Francisco

Today you reach San Francisco and should dedicate part of your day to taking pictures of the Golden Gate Bridge and driving across it. Then, you could also stroll around Fisherman's Wharf and relax in a garden.

Day 15: San Francisco

Another day in this colorful city where dense fog is a common visitor. Check out the flower power district around Haight and Ashbury, fill your belly in Chinatown, and ride a cable car. If you want, you can already start driving toward Yosemite today, to have more time in that impressive national park.

Day 16: Yosemite

The drive from San Francisco to Yosemite takes about 3.5 hours. Once at the park, take the valley loop drive and marvel at the high mountains that tower above you and the crashing waterfalls. Decide whether you want to do some hikes or do some more scenic drives to lookout points.
Spend the night near Yosemite National Park or already start driving toward Sacramento, in order to have less stress tomorrow.

Day 17: Drive-through trees

The whole way from Yosemite to Eureka would take 8.5 hours. Since today you have the opportunity to drive through tall Redwood Trees, and gawk up even more trees along the Avenue of the Giants, you should plan for a long day. Eureka would be a charming place to spend the night and then, you'd also be back at a lovely beach.

Day 18: Coastal Highway and interstate route

Have a relaxing morning at the beach in Eureka and then start the last bit of your road trip along the coast. Your destination today is Portland in the state of Oregon.

Day 19: Portland

Spend most of the day in Portland. Walk along the river and visit a botanical garden. In the late afternoon or evening, drive to Seattle in order to have a full day there.

Day 20: Seattle

This city in Washington has a lot to offer. You should check out the MoPop museum. Then, watch the boats and salmon at the Ballard Locks. Stroll through Pike Place Market and perhaps take the elevator up to the viewing platform of the Space Needle.

Day 21: Return flight

If your flight is late in the day, all the better because you have more time to explore the hip city of Seattle. Sit down and drink a coffee (maybe in the first Starbucks in the world?) or enjoy another donut while remembering all the amazing places you have seen in the past weeks.

This is a possible three-week trip on which you could manage to see all the highlights along the West Coast of the US including the best national parks. Now, let's look at the individual places in a bit more detail.

Las Vegas, Nevada

Let's start in this sparkling city where every hotel is an amusement park on its own. Las Vegas is much more than a place for gamblers. You will find replicas of important sights from around the world or from the US and hence it's a great place to start your sightseeing tour of the USA! Hotels are cheaper than in other cities, but you will have a nice room with a special decoration. There are several shopping outlets situated around Las Vegas and hence you might not even have time to set foot inside a casino. However, it's always very hot during the day, so you will actually be glad that life in Las Vegas takes place indoors in the casinos or while you enjoy a delicious meal at one of the many all-you-can-eat restaurants.

How to get from the airport to the strip

In case you are not picking up your rental car at the airport the cheapest option to get to the famous Las Vegas strip (where all the big-name casinos are located) is by bus. Buses leave from terminal 1 and terminal 3 and you best have exact change ready to purchase your ticket.

The cheapest option is Centennial Express Bus (CX) which drives past the Premium Outlets and brings you all the way to downtown Las Vegas in about 30 minutes for $2. From there, you can walk to the strip although it's probably not pleasant in this heat. Or you get off at the stop *Tropicana and Las Vegas*. There, you are close to MGM, Mandalay Bay, and Luxor.

If you don't want to walk much and, in addition, cover some comfortable Las Vegas sightseeing, purchase either a 2-hour ($6) or 24h ($8) bus pass. Take bus 109 to the South Strip Transfer Terminal in about 15 minutes and change onto a Deuce bus there. The Deuce bus runs up and down the strip 24/7. Instead of simply using it to get to your hotel, you will have a climatized transport to enjoy looking at all the hotels along the strip plus driving past the famous Las Vegas sign. Of course, you could get off to take a picture and then continue with the next bus.

What to do in Las Vegas

Whether you want to gamble, watch a show in the evening, go shopping or just hang out by the hotel pool, there is something for everyone in Las Vegas.

Gamble and drink for "free"

While the different hotels offer various incredible sights, their casinos are pretty much the same from the inside. Usually, it's a brightly lit hall with many blinking slot machines that make (rather annoying) sounds. Then, there are the table games like roulette, blackjack, or poker. For roulette and blackjack, there usually is a minimum bet of $5-$10 per round. Hence, you could lose a lot of money within minutes.

If you haven't really gambled at casinos yet and rather want to learn something, you could find a table where you can play for $1 per round. Of course, then your winnings will be less too, but at least you can spend more time playing. Unfortunately, this year, there doesn't seem to be such cheap table games along the strip. If you don't mind wandering away from the strip for a bit, you find $1 table games at *OYO Casino* and the *Downtown Grand*.

An advantage of gambling in Las Vegas is that in most casinos, waiters will serve you free cocktails while you are playing. You simply always have to tip the waiter $1 or $2, so technically, it's not entirely free. Yet, you can still have good cocktails for hardly any money.

If you want to play at the slot machines, you probably have to upload money onto a card that you receive at the casino. Ask if they have a members' club for which you can sign up for free. Sometimes they offer free slot money when signing up. Once you are done playing, you can cash out leftover money, if you have any.

Visit the best attractions along the strip

The strip refers to a section of big and famous casinos along Las Vegas Boulevard. To lure willing gamblers into their casinos and restaurants, the hotels all have special attractions that you can visit. Awesome about this is that most of them are entirely free! Hence, you could have a really entertaining time in Las Vegas without spending any money (as long as you aren't attracted by the slot machines or table games).

You won't be able to see everything that Las Vegas has to offer but here are my twelve top recommendations that you shouldn't miss. Let's start out in the heat and **take a picture of the famous "Welcome to Las Vegas" sign**. Either you ride there with the Deuce bus, or you walk from Mandalay Bay in about 15 minutes.

You will see many blinking signs in Las Vegas, but this definitely is the most iconic one.

Back at the strip, **watch the fountain show at the *Bellagio*** which starts every 15 to 30 minutes and is accompanied by music. This might be nicer when it's lit up at night. Also at the Bellagio is a nice **botanical garden with a conservatory** that is newly decorated on many occasions throughout the year. Plus, the lobby of the Bellagio is decorated with hundreds of glass flowers and there is a huge chocolate fountain. The chocolate is used for the desserts at their restaurants and hence, the Bellagio might be a good address to have a meal.

At *Mandalay Bay,* there is an **aquarium and a big lagoon**. Not an aquarium but a cute setting along canals can be found at the **Grand Canal of Venice**. You don't have to go to Italy to see the gondoliers in their striped shirts. Further, you should **take a picture of the LOVE sign** in front of the waterfall inside the *Grand Canal Shoppes* at Palazzo.

At *Circus Circus,* you can catch a **free circus performance**. They take place from the afternoon to the evening at half past the hour. **Watch the Lake of Dreams show** at the *Wynn*. It starts every half hour in the evening and is best viewed from the free visitor platform inside the hotel.

NYNY has done an excellent job at replicating famous NYC neighborhoods. Plus, there sometimes are **free dueling piano concerts** at the *Times Square Bar*. Speaking of famous cities, you also have to **watch the Eiffel Tower** sparkle at the *Paris Las Vegas* hotel in the evening. It's almost like the real one.

Visit the **contemporary art installations** inside the *Cosmopolitan*. The modern lobby with the colorful video cubes is worth a visit alone.

Finally, let your mouth water at **Hershey's Chocolate World or at the M&M world**. Two huge chocolate shops where surely everyone will find something to their taste.

Ride the free tram

Some casinos offer free shuttle trams to other casinos. If you want to visit several places along the strip, this is a convenient way to travel without having to go out into the heat. Casinos with access to free shuttles are Mandalay Bay, Excalibur, Luxor, Treasure Island, the Mirage, Bellagio, Aria, Park MGM, and the Crystals shopping center.

Fill your belly at an all-you-can-eat buffet

The all-you-can-eat buffets in Las Vegas are a food lover's dream! You will find anything your stomach craves for. Meaning: tender steak cuts, crab legs, clams or oysters, sushi, pizza, typical Asian dishes, cold cuts, salads, and various desserts from ice cream to pretty cake pops. Usually, there is a breakfast or brunch time, lunch, and dinner. You can even buy all-day eating passes for around $60-$70.

Lunches cost between $19 and $25 while dinner usually costs between $29 and $50, depending on how fancy the buffet is. A high-end choice would be the buffet at the Bellagio with chocolate fondue as a dessert option. A cheaper place but one I loved the last time I was there was the *A. Y. C. E. Buffet at the Palms* resort.

Hunt for bargains from well-known brands

There are some fashion shopping malls located inside the casinos along the strip, for example at *The Forum Shops* at Caesar's Palace, *The Grand Canal Shoppes* at Venice, or at *Fashion Show* Las Vegas. However, there the items will have normal prices or simple seasonal discounts. If you are looking for better discounts, head to *Las Vegas North Premium Outlets* (organized like an outdoor boardwalk) or *Las Vegas South Premium Outlets* (organized like a strip mall).

To the South Outlet, you get by Deuce bus or bus #117 or 217. The North Outlets you can reach with the free Downtown Loop Bus (stops include: Bonneville Transit Center, The Arts District, Arts District South, Brewery Row, Pawn Plaza, Mob Museum, Fremont Street Experience, Symphony Park, The Strat Hotel, Circa Hotel, and City Hall), or the Centennial Express, or Deuce. The North Outlets have more upscale brands while the South Outlets have a broader variety of shops. Either way, you will be able to satisfy your shopping needs.

However, if you have time after a visit to the national parks, you could stop at the *Prizm Outlets in Primm* about 40 minutes from Las Vegas by car. I liked them 15 years ago but now I wouldn't go out of my way to drive there because the outlets in Las Vegas are more modern.

Now you have plenty to do while you visit Las Vegas. Before you start a road trip to the national parks, you should take the opportunity and stock up on snacks and water in a Walmart or some other big supermarket.

Route 66

This road is also a symbol of the American dream and freedom as it was one of the first roads that connected the states in the center of the US with the West Coast. It covered the distance between Chicago and Santa Monica in LA. While the road actually ends in downtown Los Angeles, you can find the end of the road sign at the Santa Monica Pier.

Nowadays, Route 66 is too narrow and curvy to cater to the many cars and trucks. Therefore, it often runs parallel to bigger highways and isn't really marked on the maps anymore. Yet, in California or Nevada, you still have several chances to get off the highway and actually drive on route 66. For example, when heading to the Grand Canyon South Rim, you can get on Route 66 at *Kingman* and back on the highway after *Seligman*.

Visiting the National Parks along the West Coast of the USA

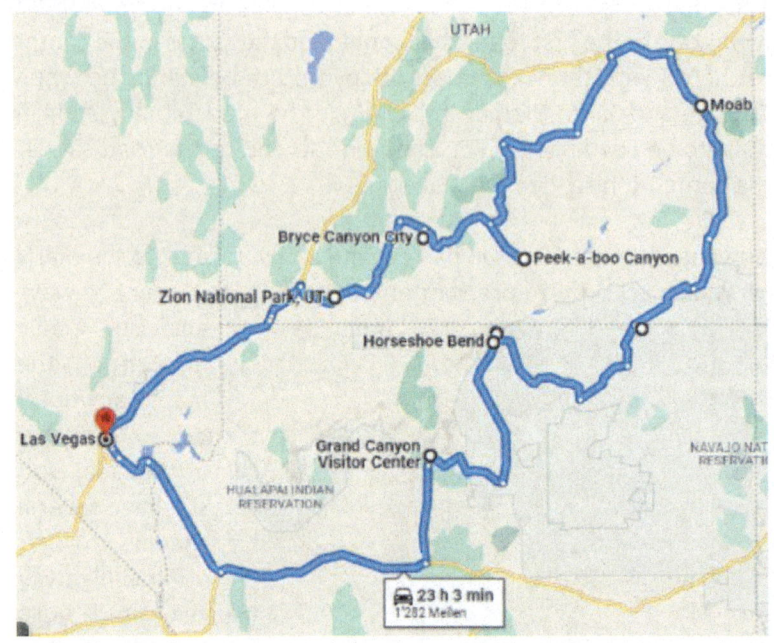

Map: This is what your tour of the national parks in the Southwest looks like.

The big-name national parks all have an entry fee of around $30-$35 per vehicle. If you arrive on foot, they charge a bit less but therefore, per person. The good news is that they offer an **annual park card which costs $80**. Even if you only travel for one week, if you visit three parks, it will already have been worth the purchase. Plus, who knows, you might come back for more nature in the same year. The pass covers parks across the whole US, including Alaska. You can buy the **America the Beautiful** annual pass at all the entrance gates to the national parks. Make sure that you don't accidentally buy an annual pass simply for one national park like Zion or Grand Canyon.

While touring the national parks in this area, be sure to glance up to the night sky every evening. You will spend the night in some very remote places with hardly any light pollution. Some national parks even extra make sure of this. Therefore, you can enjoy incredible views of the stars!

Grand Canyon

The Grand Canyon keeps what its name promises. It's an incredibly vast area of deep gorges with nice color hues. On the edges of the canyon, you have spectacular views and can witness stunning sunrises or sunsets.

Since there is no bridge crossing the Grand Canyon (you would need about a 16 km long bridge for that), you can choose between two entry points to get into Grand Canyon National Park: the North Rim or the South Rim. Perhaps, you have also heard of *Grand Canyon West*. That part doesn't belong to the national park but is an adventure area managed by the Hualapai Tribe. Their cheapest ticket costs $77 per person and the only difference is that you can walk on a glass-bottom bridge above the canyon. You then still need the national park ticket if you want to see Grand Canyon at the other entry points.

The South Rim

This is the more touristy developed part where you find many amazing viewing platforms, as well as convenient facilities. Plus, you could rent a bike with *Bright Angel Bicycles* or take a trip on a mule. Renting a bike seems like a spectacular thing to do in this place. You can rent it close to the visitor center starting at as little as $12 with a free shuttle transport back so that you only have to ride in one direction. Unfortunately, like most visitors, I didn't have time for this last time and simply drove by car to one viewing platform after the other, which of course, was amazing as well.

Some of the famous viewpoints are *Mather Point, Grandview*, and the *Desert View Watchtower*. We also saw several elks along the drive.

You could spend the night in the town of Tusayan, very close to the entry point. If you want to stay inside the park, you will have to be very early with making a reservation. Perhaps even a whole year in advance.

If you have more time, you could attempt one of the hikes in the park. Just be aware that it gets really hot in summer. Bring plenty of water. A nice path is *Bright Angel Trail* which will eventually lead down to the Colorado River. However, better don't go this far if you just want to enjoy the view and turn around with enough energy to get back up to your car.

If you have some hiking experience and know your fitness level, you could do the *rim-to-rim hike*. It connects South Kaibab Trail with the North Kaibab Trail. It's 21 miles (34 km) from South to North with long and steep ascends, and you will need 9-13 hours for it. So, perhaps, you have to take additional preparations in order that you can camp somewhere in the canyon (for example at Phantom Ranch Lodge). Once you arrive at the other rim, you can take a pre-booked shuttle (www.trans-canyonshuttle.com/rim-to-rim-shuttle-schedules) back to the other canyon. This drive takes about 4.5 hours, just like if you want to visit both canyon entrances and drive from the South to the North Rim yourself.

The North Rim

This part feels more remote with fewer people and more forest. Perhaps because you share the views with less tourists, they might blow you away even more. Here, popular viewing platforms are *Bright Angel Point*, *Point Imperial,* and *Cape Royal.* Be aware that due to snow, the North Rim is closed between mid-October and mid-May. Check the website of the Grand Canyon for the exact opening dates: www.nps.gov/grca/planyourvisit/index.htm.
We drove to Cape Royal from where we walked to Angel's Window and then had lunch in the shade of the trees close to an outdoor chapel on the brim of the canyon.
On the third attempt, we finally spotted the starting point of the *Cliff Springs walk.* That was really cool with orange overhanging cliffs and the path was often shaded by trees. Even children would like to go hiking in this terrain. It's a real adventure.
In the end, we drove to Cape Imperial. From there, Grand Canyon looks never-ending, spreading along the whole horizon.

Another more difficult, but short hike (about 1.5 km) to start and assess how you feel is toward *Ooh-Aah Point*. You could then continue to *Cedar Ridge* but just remember that you will have to climb out of the canyon again.

Page (Arizona) with Horseshoe Bend, Lake Powell, and Antelope Canyon

You left the state of Nevada and now have arrived in Arizona. Page is a small town, but you find big supermarkets and many restaurants to stock up on any kind of supplies that you might need. There are campgrounds and hotels to choose from.
Near Page, you can find several stunning tourist sights.

Horseshoe Bend

Probably, you have already seen a picture of this incredible place where the insanely blue-green Colorado river circles around a big, brown rock. The contrast of the sand brown rock and the water makes the color play all the more intense.

You get to the lookout point by driving for about 6 minutes from Page to *Horseshoe Bend Overlook Parking Lot*, which is marked on Google Maps. There, you walk up a dune for 5-10 minutes. Better wear closed shoes as the sand can be quite hot. Then, you reach the canyon rim and can enjoy the view! Just don't go too close to the edge simply to get that selfie...When I was there the first time, there were no fences, however, nowadays it seems to be necessary to have them.

After coming here when you arrive in Page, you might want to come back the next day for sunrise, just because it is such a picturesque spot and so easily accessible.

Lake Powell

Lake Powell offers picturesque views since it's actually a canyon that was filled with water and now brings power to Glen Canyon Dam. The Lake Powell area is also a national park which would cost $25 to enter but is included in the *America the Beautiful* annual pass. So, head past the viewpoint of Glen Canyon Dam toward *Wahweap Marina*. Along the drive, you pass several nice viewpoints of the lake. If you want to swim, follow the *Coves Loop*. There you have three small beaches. The last one is sandy. You are not allowed to swim in the marina, but you could rent a boat and explore the lake with more secluded beaches.

There are no lifeguards along the water and the water might be quite cold. Therefore, be careful when entering it and don't just jump from a cliff. First of all, because your body might get a shock if it was overheated before, and secondly you don't know if there are rocks below the surface if you can't see to the bottom of the lake. Due to global warming, there now sometimes are very low water levels and many boat docking points even have to close.

Antelope Canyon

This is one of the most beautiful canyons on earth and has definitely won many prizes for photographers. You will walk in a narrow gorge with smooth, winding rocks. The rocks shine in a warm orange and white and depending on how the sun falls into the canyon, it almost becomes a magical place.

The downside is that you can only visit it with a Navajo tour guide and the fees are not included in the national park pass.

Antelope Canyon has two parts that can be visited, the Upper Antelope Canyon and the Lower Antelope Canyon. If you plan your day ahead, you can manage to visit both. Antelope Canyon is located 10 minutes West of Page in the *Lake Powell Navajo Tribal Park.* Your tour either begins in Page or at the entry point off Highway 98. You have to arrive at least 15 minutes before your tour starts. A 4WD will then bring you to the canyon entrance. The Upper Antelope Canyon is a pretty much even footpath. In the Lower Antelope Canyon, you will have to climb down a steep latter into the canyon. Because of this, more people visit the Upper Antelope Canyon since it's easier. Be sure to check the following website early enough in order to book your guided tour: https://navajonationparks.org/guided-tour-operators/antelope- canyon-tour-operators/

Prices range from $50 to $90 per person for a 1.5-hour tour and $40 to $80 for a 1h tour, depending on whether it is a normal tourist tour or a photography tour. Despite those prices, I would say that it's like with Machu Picchu; Antelope Canyon is a place you just have to visit if you are nearby.

Alternatives to Antelope Canyon

If you feel discouraged because of those prices anyway, there are some canyons in Utah that look similar to Antelope Canyon. You find them in the *Grand Staircase-Escalante National Monument.* For example, Paria Canyon, about 1 hour from Page. For this one, you only need a permit to visit it which costs $6. Or Wire Pass to Buckskin Gulch hike which is also located about 1 hour North of Page. More options you have near Bryce Canyon in Utah like Peek-A-Boo, Spooky Gulches, and Zebra Slot Canyon.

With all those options, you have to be a fit adventurer. First, you have to plan the hikes and obtain the required permits yourself. Further, the terrain is difficult, and you might have to rock climb or wade through shin to hip-high water. Hence, you need good equipment as well. Moreover, bumpy roads lead to the hiking trails, and depending on the conditions, they might only be accessible with a 4WD. So, if you have a 4WD and time, I would definitely go and check out at least one of the trails and just see how far you are comfortable with heading inside the canyons.

More details about the hikes near Page as well as the hikes near Escalante you find in the chapter about the *Grand Staircase-Escalante National Monument (p. 60).*

Monument Valley

Monument Valley is a landscape with plateau rocks in an otherwise flat, dry scenery. The rocks come in different shapes, and we recognize them right away because they have been the setting in several movies, for example during the jogging phase of Forrest Gump. There now even is a spot marked on Google Maps called Forrest Gump Point on Highway 163. It's this long stretch of straight road with the iconic rock plateaus in the background. This view, you can have for free.

If you want to see more of the Monument Valley, you have to enter Monument Valley Navajo Tribal Park, which is not included in the national park pass. The entry fee is $8 per person. Inside the Tribal Park, you can drive the unpaved 17 mi (27 km) Tribal Park Loop. It's recommended to do it with a 4WD as your rental car insurance probably doesn't cover damage if you have a problem on unpaved roads. However, if it hasn't rained and since everyone drives slow on this scenic route anyway, your car should be fine.

Otherwise, you could also opt for a guided tour where a Navajo guide will take you on a 3h tour of the valley. You can book the tours at the visitor center, online, or in a nearby hotel. On the 3h tour, you will also see places that aren't accessible without a guide. Prices are around $80 per person.

An even more fun way to see the valley is on a 2h horseback riding trip which can also be booked at the visitor center. However, it costs around $110 per person and when we got there, the tours were booked up until sunset. Since we didn't want to wait half a day, we didn't do the ride. So, if you think that's something you really want to do, you could pre-book a tour on this website: https://discovernavajo.com/horseback-tours/

From here, you will continue your drive toward Moab, the closest town to Arches National Park. This drive is incredibly scenic, and you should plan many roadside stops to take pictures of the landscape!

Arches National Park

This national park will impress you with, as the name hints, big stone arches. They were built naturally through erosion. Especially in the soft morning or afternoon light, the orange color of the arches truly stands out.

You can do different walks in the park and visit various formations. Since there also are short walks available, this park is suitable for every visitor. Perhaps, you will be glad to do a short hike, too, because it can get incredibly hot between the rocks or while being exposed to the sun. Bear that in mind and bring a hat and water!

Plus, the weather can change quickly from sunshine to a storm, by when you should be arriving back at your car. The park also looks pretty in winter with snow. Then, you can even manage to hike during the warmest hours of the day, while this is a bad idea in summer.

Entering the national park is free with the *America the Beautiful* pass.

The three best hikes to see a bit of everything

1. Windows Primitive Loop

I liked this section in the park the best since the hike is easy and short and you can walk right below the massive stone arches. Plus, the scenery looks a bit different as there are also some green plants.
The loop hike is only 1 mi (1.6 km) long and will take you to North Window, Turret Arch, and South Window.
Don't climb inside the South Window since people have fallen down or gotten stranded and also, you might damage the arches if you touch them (and millions of visitors each year do the same).

2. Landscape Arch

This is a thin, delicate arch that spans a big distance. Hence, it's quite impressive and also has a time limit since it will most likely get destroyed if there is an earthquake.
You can get there by walking an easy trail which is 1.6 miles (2.5 km) roundtrip. On the way to Landscape Arch, you have the option to add 15 minutes to your hike by also visiting Pine Tree Arch and Tunnel Arch. Those sights are well worth the detour before walking back up to the Landscape Arch trail.

3. Delicate Arch

This is the biggest free-standing arch in the park. If you only want to take a look at it from further away, walk 100 m on an even path to get to the first viewpoint. 800 m down the path and up some stairs, you get to the Upper Viewpoint with a less obstructed view. If you want to get closer to the arch, it gets trickier. The whole round trip is 3 mi (4.8 km) and will take you 2-3 hours. It's not difficult because of its length but because there are steep ascents on slippery hard rock and the heat makes everything tougher on your body.

A scenic drive

When leaving Arches National Park and driving toward Bryce Canyon, you must take Byway 12 which leaves Route 24 in Torrey. Between here and Bryce this scenic road was voted the second most beautiful driving route in the world by *foxnews.com*.
And this after having been impressed on the drive between Monument Valley and Moab. What more is there to come?
You pass stunning, rocky landscape with more arches visible from the road and even drive through tunnel arches.
In case you wondered, the first road on *foxnews*'s list was Milford Road in New Zealand.

Grand Staircase-Escalante National Monument

This isn't simply a small visitor spot to check off your list but actually, it's a huge area in Utah that covers an amazing landscape with many treasures. It's called staircase because big plateaus descend naturally and apart from additional stone arches, everything shines in a beautiful color mix.

Hence, you can take in a lot of the beauty simply by driving the roads in the Grand Staircase-Escalante National Monument area, for example, Byway 12.

If you want to get closer to the sights or even hike a sloth canyon (here's where you find the good alternatives to Antelope Canyon!), you need to leave the paved roads though. If you are serious about doing hikes in this area, you should come with a 4WD. In case you are more spontaneous, you could simply check what conditions the roads leading to the trailheads are currently in. If you feel comfortable driving them in a normal car (which can be possible) you can try it!

The top things to do

Here, you can visit high waterfalls or do hikes that you will remember your whole life.

Wire Pass to Buckskin Gulch hike

This one is actually located one hour from Page, Arizona, and is better accessed from there. It's easier compared to the canyon hikes around Escalante and therefore more advisable if you aren't familiar with climbing and canyoning.

First, follow highway 89 from Page until you reach the turn-off to House Rock Valley Road. Follow this unpaved road for about 8.4

mi (13 km) until you reach the spacious parking lot of the Wire Pass Trailhead.

You need to purchase a day-pass for $6 beforehand online: www.recreation.gov/activitypass/10006177

Although this hike doesn't involve actual rock climbing, it still leads across loose, big rocks for which you need good shoes. Also don't start this hike if there is the smallest chance of rain, since rain can quickly turn into a deadly flood in a canyon.

Apart from those dangers, this hike is absolutely spectacular and can be done in 1.5-2 hours. The round-trip distance is 3.4 mi (5.4 km).

Lower Calf Creek Falls

Normally, I am a big waterfall lover and since we haven't seen any waterfalls on this trip yet, you might want to take this easily accessible hike near Escalante. The trail starts at the Calf Creek campground along Scenic Byway 12. The hike to the falls is 2.5 mi (4 km) and you come back the same way. The water falls 126 feet (38 m).

For this hike, you don't need a permit if you have the annual national park pass. Otherwise, it's $5 per car.

The slot canyons

Unfortunately, I didn't have time to attempt those hikes and the possible need for a 4WD put us off as well. However, the scenery is spectacular in Peek-a-boo Gulch and Spooky Gulch canyons, as well as Zebra Slot Canyon and Willis Creek Slot Canyon. The latter is the easiest hike of the canyon hikes.

To get a better idea of all of these places and look at more pictures, check out the informative page by Brycecanyoncountry.com: www.brycecanyoncountry.com/blog/post/the-grand-staircase-slot-canyons-peek-a-boo-and-spooky-gulch/

Staying in Escalante

The small town of Escalante is a charming place to stay, even if you aren't doing any activities in this area but are on your way to Bryce Canyon. Also, prices here were cheaper than in the other areas where we camped/stayed.

Bryce Canyon

This is one of my favorite places in the world because it simply looks like a fantasy world from another planet. Bryce Canyon is filled with rock pillars, called hoodoos, which look as if somebody had dripped a lot of sand on the spot of each pillar. To make it even better, the usually orange sand is colored with light brown, white, and red hues.

In winter, it can snow in Bryce Canyon which makes everything appear even more magical.
It's included in the *America the beautiful* park pass.

The main thing to do in Bryce Canyon is to drive the 18 miles (29 km) long Southern Scenic Drive where you can stop at 9 viewpoints.
My favorite one is *Bryce Point*.
Apart from simply driving, you should get out of the car and marvel at the hoodoos from up close. The most popular hike is a loop hike from Sunrise Point to Sunset Point. You descend via Queen's Garden trail that then turns into Navajo Loop trail. Once you arrive at Sunset Point, you walk back to Sunrise Point along the rim for 0.5 mi (0.8 km). The whole hike is 2.9 mi (4.6 km), and you will need 2-3 hours.

Zion National Park

Zion National Park is different from the other parks in Utah because the red gorge is also covered with a rich, green flora. Therefore, it looks like a peaceful paradise. It's a truly beautiful place where you can enjoy many picturesque views.

In addition, no cars are allowed in the national park. You will leave it at the parking lot at the entrance and then either walk to the start of your trail or take one of the many free shuttles that bring people to the trailheads. Because of this, there is a much bigger chance of seeing animals, since they don't have to hide from tourist cars. I've seen deer, chipmunks (cute!), and a tarantula (eeeew!).
The *America the Beautiful* pass is valid here.

The most popular hike is called Angel's Landing. It's so breathtakingly beautiful, that I've actually done it twice (in different years) and unfortunately haven't seen much else of the park yet. However, sadly, since 2022 you need a permit for this hike, and it's organized as a lottery. That makes planning this hike very unpredictable.

It works like this, that you have to apply for the permit between 12.01 a.m. and 3 p.m. on the day before you wish to hike. Applying costs $6 per group and in case you don't get the permit, you won't be refunded the money but can apply again. If you get the permit, you will receive an e-mail by 4 p.m. and will have to pay $3 per person. You can apply here: www.nps.gov/zion/planyourvisit/angels-landing-hiking-permits.htm

Don't be too disappointed if you don't get a permit. There are many nice easy and moderate hikes in Zion National Park, and you could even decide spontaneously at the visitor center, which one attracts you most. Or check them out on the national park's website beforehand: www.nps.gov/zion/planyourvisit/zion-canyon-trail-descriptions.htm

The hike to Angel's Landing

You take the shuttle bus to *#6 The Grotto*. The round-trip distance is 5.4 mi / 8.7 km, and you will ascend/descend 1,488 ft / 453 m. The hike will take you 3-4 hours with breaks.

The beginning of the hike is easy on a concrete path. Afterward, there follows a steep zig-zag path, but we were very surprised by how quickly we arrived at the top. We had planned for a very strenuous experience like the description had said but there was no way we'd need four hours for this. Well, we weren't at the top yet. Now the fun part of climbing along the mountain crest began. There was a metal chain to hold on to. You wouldn't want to be up here during a storm. There was a 400m cliff straight to the bottom of the valley on each side of us. Hence, you shouldn't do this hike if you are afraid of heights. Yet, the views down into the valley are absolutely stunning. It looks like a place where dinosaurs could still be alive and poke their heads up in between the trees.

Once at the top, take a seat and be sure to enjoy the view.

Then, you return to the bus stop slowly and steadily. Perhaps you even have time to do a second trail. Perhaps one where you simply walk on a straight, even path this time.

Death Valley

The Death Valley is the driest place in the US and also has the lowest elevation at 282 feet (86 m) below sea level. Some otherworldly landscapes can be seen in this national park which is also included in the America the Beautiful pass. Therefore, it's well worth the 2-hour drive from Las Vegas instead of heading directly to LA or San Diego.

What to see

Simply by driving through the Death Valley, you will already see different landscapes. Bear in mind that it gets extremely hot here during the day. Hence, if you want to get out of the car to visit one of the following four main sights, you want to be at Death Valley early or late in the day.

Artists Palette is a rock valley, where someone seems to have dusted the mountains with splashes of color. I am not talking about the usual reds, oranges, and whites but about blues and greens! So, this is definitely an unusual place to visit.
The second place you should get out of your car is **Badwater Basin**. Those are salt flats where you could take funny perspective shots if you walk out far enough. However, since it's so hot, best bring a light scarf to cover your face and shoulders, wear a hat with a broad brim and bring water.
The third recommended stop is **Zabriskie Point** which reminded me of Bryce Canyon but without the hoodoos and a smoother, rigged surface instead. This one is especially picturesque for sunset, watching the colors of the sky and the orange and pink on the rocks change. Another cool stop is the

Mesquite Flat Sand Dunes. It's awesome to look at a landscape that makes you feel as if you landed in the Sahara Desert. You can see some of the dunes from the parking lot but for better pictures, you should follow the hiking trail up the dunes. However, the national park website advises that you don't hike on the dunes after 10 a.m. because it's too hot. So, if you want to explore the Death Valley, you need to be a very early riser for one day or best already spend the night before at the national park. The Death Valley is another perfect location for stargazing.

To visit the four locations with small hikes and drive through the valley will take you about 3 hours.

Now, we leave the national parks of the Southwest and travel toward the beautiful West Coast.

San Diego

If I could pick a place to live in the USA, it would be San Diego. It has perfect weather, many beautiful beaches for swimming surfing, and wildlife watching, picturesque old town sections, delicious restaurants or food carts, and entertaining parks. You could easily spend a whole week of holidays here, so with only one or two days, you have to make cuts and decide which of the following things to do attracts you most.

How to get from the airport to the city center

In case you don't travel by rental car, you can reach the city center by taxi in 15 minutes (about $25) or by public bus 992, which takes 20 minutes and costs $2. The bus operates from 4.50 a.m. to midnight, and you can check which stop is most convenient for you on Google or the moovitapp: https://moovitapp.com/

The best things to do in San Diego

This list could be much longer but to get a great feeling for San Diego and its various attractions, you should try to make time for the following places.

Swim, snorkel, or surf at the most picturesque beaches

Especially the beaches at **La Jolla** are famous for being beautiful and having something in store for everyone. At La Jolla Shores Park, the water is most easily accessible and therefore the best place for families to swim or snorkel. Then, there are more secluded coves, where you might see wildlife while snorkeling. We've even seen many leopard sharks in the water. Apparently, they are not dangerous because people treat them respectfully and keep their distance.

For longer stretches of sand head to Mission Beach or Pacific Beach. At **Mission Beach**, you can stroll along the boardwalk or take a breezy bike ride. Children and people with a sweet tooth will enjoy **Belmont Park** at Mission Beach, where you find fair rides and booths selling sweets or fast food.

North Pacific Beach is a long stretch of sand that is supervised by lifeguards.

Watch seals at the Children's Pool Beach

This beach is also located in La Jolla and had been constructed so that children could swim safely shielded from the big waves. However, seals and sea lions seem to have thought of this as an invitation and since then come to birth their babies here between December to May. Then, it's not advisable to go down to the beach but you can watch them from the sea wall.

Visit the San Diego Zoo

This zoo is known as one of the best zoos in the world and I really enjoyed my visit there. The animal habitats are spacious, and the layout is practical for visitors. You can see many endangered animals like giant pandas, polar bears, and koalas.

For this visit, you should plan at least 4-5 hours, and then you could combine it with strolling through Balboa Park since that's where the zoo is located.

Unfortunately, ticket prices are very expensive at $63 for people above 12 years old (if you buy the ticket online: https://zoo.sandiegozoo.org/tickets). Apart from being able to see so many animals, the ticket does include buses, and an aerial tram inside the zoo, so you don't have to cover all the distances on foot.

Explore Balboa Park

This big park is home to many incredibly beautiful gardens, a huge and picturesque plant house, and many other picturesque buildings in the Spanish colonial style. Just by looking at the free things in this park you can spend several hours there. If you also want to visit some of the paid museums or the San Diego Zoo, you could spend several days here.

Enjoy a sunset at Sunset Cliffs Park

This park near Point Loma keeps the promise of offering you stunning sunset views. In addition, you have the chance of spotting gray whales between December and April, so be sure to scan the water surface for fins or water splashes.

Fill your belly with a delicious meal

Being located so close to the border of Mexico, authentic Mexican cuisine has made it to San Diego. You really can't go wrong with tacos, burritos, or quesadillas and guacamole here. My favorite restaurant was **Pokéz** (www.pokezsd.com/). They even offer vegetarian or vegan options.

A good piece of advice for San Diego is to look out for food trucks since you can encounter delicious treasures there as well.

In the iconic street of **Little Italy,** you can stroll through Saturday's Farmers' Market along Date Street, between Kettner Boulevard and Front Street. On any other day, it's also a nice area for a café, beer, or pizza.

A covered market that is open daily from 11 a.m. to 7 p.m. is **Liberty Public Market**. There you find local delicacies, art, as well as food stalls.

Go out in the Gaslamp Quarter

In downtown San Diego near Petco Park and the Convention Center, you find a few charming streets with lots of historical buildings and pretty streetlamps. This is the best area for a night out. We enjoyed an amazing piano/singing duel.

In case you are in San Diego during a festival like Mardi Gras or St. Patrick's Day, this is where a street party would take place.

Visit the charming San Diego Old Town

Don't confuse this part with "downtown" San Diego. I really mean the Old Town. It's a picturesque area with historical buildings where you feel like you have landed directly in an old Western movie. It's definitely worth taking a stroll in this area and having a meal here.

Ride the Pacific Surfliner to Los Angeles

Here, it actually is an advantage if you don't travel by car because you won't miss out on this picturesque train ride. Especially in San Diego and Orange County, you can enjoy direct views of the Pacific Ocean through the window. Sit on the left side when riding toward LA.
There are special racks for surfboards, and you could choose any surf beach location to get off along the way.
This train also takes you to Anaheim (where you change onto line 15 to get to Disneyland) in 2 hours, or to Downtown L.A. in 3 hours.

Los Angeles

Known as L. A. the biggest city in California is linked to fun beach life and the movie world. You could spend days on tours through movie studios, past private homes of famous stars, or by finding their names on the walk of fame. Apart from that, you can marvel at modern architecture in downtown L.A. and visit many great art galleries. So, Los Angeles isn't just a city with a big airport and a good tourist marketing. It really is a great place to visit!

How to get from the airport to the city center

The cheapest airfare you find will likely bring you to LAX. Unfortunately, the highways to get you downtown in your rental car or taxi (about $60), or Uber (about $30) are congested with traffic from 5 a.m. to 11 p.m. and it will take between 25 to 45 minutes to get to the city center.

Cheaper options are to travel by *FlyAway Bus* directly from the airport to Union Station for $10 per person. This will take about 35 minutes.
It's even cheaper if you take the free LAX G Shuttle to Aviation/LAX Station. There you switch onto Metro line C (Green) which will bring you downtown. It costs $1.75 per person but you have to purchase a metro card for $2 if you don't have one yet. This method of transportation takes about 1 hour for reaching the city center.

The best things to do in L.A.

Whether you are here to people watch on Rodeo Drive, go shopping, enjoy art, or bodysurf in the ocean, you will probably want to come back for more in the future.
For everything in the city center area, see whether you can reach it conveniently by bus as parking can be very expensive.

Enjoy California's beach scene

At the picturesque and iconic **Santa Monica Pier** you can enjoy the rides of the theme park which you can enter for free and pay for each ride separately, all while having a view of the beach. In addition, there is a shopping center close to the beach with well-known brands and nice cafés (**Third Street Promenade**). After having taken some photos of the pier, the **Route 66 end of the trail** sign, and having eaten a corn dog, you should head down to the beach along which you will surely find a perfect spot for your towel, the further away you go from the pier.

From Santa Monica to Malibu, you should drive the very picturesque stretch of the **Pacific Coastal Highway**. In Malibu, there are many good beaches to choose from. Among the favorites of the locals are **Zuma Beach** (secluded and clean but good access by car), **Westward Beach** (many lifeguards), and **Surfrider Beach** (good for surfing or watching surfers).
Then, of course, there is **Venice Beach**. It's a very picturesque, long beach but above all, it's known for the many roller skaters. Close to Venice Beach you also find a charming quarter with canals. It's a residential area that's very inviting for a stroll.

In case the waves are too choppy for you to enter, or you prefer simply looking at the ocean anyway, either take a stroll along one of the many boardwalks or rent a bicycle along the beaches in Santa Monica and ride on The Strand bike path (Marvin Braude Bike Trail). It starts at Will Rogers State Beach in Santa Monica and leads all the way down to Redondo Beach in Torrance.

Visit the best art museums

In L.A. you have the tough choice between several amazing museums and most of them are even free! Let's start with the contemporary art museum **The Broad** (https://ticketing.thebroad.org/) where you need to reserve your ticket online although it is free. Especially the Infinity Mirrored Room is immensely popular, and tickets disappear fast. It's closed on Mondays and Tuesdays.

Right across the street, there is another modern art museum, the **MOCA**. At the moment, you also have to purchase free tickets in advance online (https://moca.ticketapp.org/portal/pages/tickets). Perhaps that will change again, once COVID is in the past. In between those two museums you could have an up-close look at the Walt Disney Concert Hall which builds a triangle with those two museums.

A popular Instagram spot is the light bulb installation in front of the **LACMA** museum. In 2024 the new building for the permanent collection will open. Until then you can visit the good temporary exhibitions. You have to book the tickets online in advance. Adults cost $25 but on the second Tuesday of every month, entry is free (www.lacma.org/gettickets).

Real treasures are the **Getty Center** (closed on Monday) and the **Getty Villa Museum** (closed on Tuesday). Both can be visited for free but due to COVID also require a temporary time slot ticket (www.getty.edu/museum/). The Getty Center is a more modern building surrounded by a picturesque park. The Getty Villa is a Roman-style villa with Greek and Roman artifacts and a beautiful garden. Simply a delightful place to spend time at.

Get your Hollywood fix

Let's start with the obvious sights and head to the **Walk of Fame**. Look for the stars of your favorite actors. Then, also check taking a picture of the **Dolby Theatre** and the **TCL Chinese Theatre** off your list.

If you are interested in the homes of the stars, you could drive through **Beverly Hills** in your car. However, traffic is often slow, and you won't really see anything. If you book a "home of the stars" tour, you will at least hear some gossip about whoever currently lives there.

Obviously, you then need a perfect picture of the **Hollywood sign**. For that, head to the west side of Griffith Park and carefully drive up the winding roads to Lake Hollywood Park. From there, you have an unobstructed view of the sign and can also enjoy a green space with a playground.

Visit the most iconic buildings and places

The most spectacular building in L.A. is the **Walt Disney Concert Hall** with its stainless-steel walls that hug the building in soft waves.

L.A.'s **City Hall** isn't nearly as impressive but what many don't know is that, from Monday to Friday between 8 a.m. and 5 p.m. you can take an elevator up to the 27th floor for free and enjoy the view of the skyline of Los Angeles. You have to bring an ID or passport to be able to enter the building.

A famous road in L.A. that you shouldn't skip is **Rodeo Drive**. Walk along this luxurious street and window shop at high-end luxury brands or watch well-dressed people and observe expensive cars. Another famous road is **Sunset Boulevard** which connects downtown L.A. with Malibu. Hence, you could choose Sunset Boulevard for one way and the Pacific Coastal Highway for the way back.

Spend a day at a theme park

First, let's start with the most nostalgic park, **Disneyland Park** in Anaheim. This is the original theme park that was opened by Walt Disney. Visit the iconic castle and meet Mickey and co. Prices start at $104 for one day. In 2001 a second park, called Disney California Adventure Park was opened and you now have the option to visit both parks in one day or divide your visits across multiple days. Compare the attractions on Disneyland's website to decide which park you might enjoy more (https://disneyland.disney.go.com/destinations/disneyland/).

You can stay at a Disneyland Resort or spend the evening in the Disney village with shops and restaurants called *Downtown Disney*.

Secondly, you could experience a thrilling day at **Universal Studios**. The attractions there generally seem modern and there are many thrill rides. Plus, there is a Harry Potter section in the park, so obviously, as a Harry Potter fan, I had to go :D.

Tipp: In case you go on a water ride, mentally prepare for it that you could end up completely soaked if you don't bring a rain poncho. However, it's not too bad with California's weather.

A 1-hour studio tour is included as one of the attractions in the park. It's an entertaining tour where you receive inside knowledge about special effects while you experience them firsthand.

One-day general admission starts at $109.

The evening you can spend at *Universal CityWalk* which is a whirlwind of blinking neon signs and smells of delicious foods. This area is attractive even if you haven't spent the day in the park but just want to have a fun evening or go to the modern cinema.

Further, if you don't want to spend an entire day at a theme park or are not into rides, you could attend a movie **studio tour at**

Warner Bros. The tour takes about 3 hours and prices start at $69. You will visit several movie sets and will be able to interact with the props.

Another place where you can do a studio tour is **Paramount Pictures**. The general tour takes 2 hours and starts at $63. You will learn a lot about the history of Paramount and perhaps even see a famous person since the studios are still in use.

In case you are planning to do several touristy tours or visit theme parks, check out the **GoCity All Inclusive Pass**. It will surely bring you some savings: https://gocity.com/los-angeles/en-us/products/all-inclusive

Eat delicious food

With neighborhoods like **Chinatown**, **Korea Town**, and **Little Tokyo**, every foodie is sure to find something mouthwatering in Los Angeles. In case you are looking for a place where you find everything in one spot, head to **Grand Central Market** with food stalls from around the world. Also, as soon as you arrive in L.A. you should start your mission to find the best **taco truck**. Once more, you can enjoy very authentic and delicious Mexican food. Do you prefer sitting down? Head to the popular **Neptune's Net** seafood and burger restaurant in Malibu, from where you can enjoy a view of the ocean.

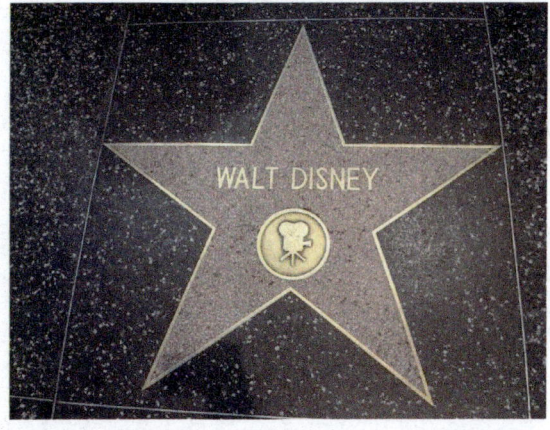

Highway #1

Highway One, mostly marked as Pacific Coast Highway is one of the most spectacular roads to drive. It starts north of San Diego and curves along the coast until north of San Francisco. Without even leaving your car, you can enjoy nearly constant incredible views of the ocean. This includes picturesque bays, long beaches, waterfalls dropping down onto a beach, wildlife far away in the water, or wildlife that has come ashore. Then, of course, you will drive through towns along the way that look exactly how you had imagined California; lively beaches with boardwalks, surfers, and cute inns and restaurants.

You are in for a treat while driving the Pacific Coast Highway. Of course, you could spread the more than 1000 km over a whole month since there are so many places worth stopping at along the way. In order to fit it into our highlights-itinerary, I only listed the absolute must-sees along Highway One in the following list.

First, three things you have to bear in mind while driving Highway One:

1. Watch the road while you are driving

The road is curvy and since it's so popular, you won't be the only driver. Therefore, if you are the one behind the wheel, it's crucial that you concentrate on driving. Don't let yourself get distracted by the views even though this is difficult. We don't want you accidentally driving off a cliff or crashing with someone else.

Luckily, there are plenty of roadside areas where you can pull over. Stop and enjoy the views and only take out your phone to take a picture when you are not driving. Switch the driver often if you aren't traveling alone, so that the rest of the passengers can look out of the window and the time of sightseeing and being concentrated is shared fairly.

2. Don't confuse the Pacific Coast Highway with Highway 101

Highway 101 sometimes runs parallel to Highway 1 but a bit more inland. Therefore, it's the quicker and more direct route to drive from south to north or vice versa. However, you won't have those amazing views on Highway 101.

3. Pay attention to the distances between gas stations

In some areas along the Pacific Coast Highway, there is more nature than civilization and you might not even have cell or radio reception. Also, the curves or ascends and descends on cliffs can empty your tank quicker than you think. Therefore, better fill up your tank a bit more often and pay attention to the signs that announce the distance to the next gas station.

Must do stops along Highway 1

A very pretty but also terribly busy stretch of Highway 1 is the part between Los Angeles and Malibu. If you haven't driven this part yet while you were visiting Los Angeles, enjoy it now! Be sure to take a break at least at one of the Malibu beaches.
Otherwise, our next stop after L.A. is Santa Barbara.

Santa Barbara, Solvang, and Pismo Beach

This town is 100 mi (160 km) from L.A. and simply the driving time is 2h. Santa Barbara is probably the image of how we imagine a beach town in California. There are long stretches of beach where people play volleyball, and swimmers and surfers are in the water. Plus, the town itself is pretty with some Spanish colonial-style architecture. Stop here to **enjoy beach life** or to visit the famous **Old Mission Santa Barbara.** It's a picturesque complex and costs

$15 to enter. I would only make time for this spot if you are interested in religious buildings and haven't been to Mexico or Spain recently, where you will have seen similar buildings.

After half a day in Santa Barbara, continue to **Solvang** (35 mi (56 km)/ 40 mins), where we have left Spanish architecture and now have arrived in a small replica of **Denmark**. Take a walk around the pretty town with the iconic **windmill**. Decide whether you want to spend the night here or rather in the beach town of **Pismo Beach**, which would mean driving another 60 miles (100 km) north.
Pismo Beach is a beautiful, long stretch of sand with a nice pier. It's a great beach to watch the sunset or go for a surf.

Morro Bay, Big Sur, Monterrey, Santa Cruz

The complete driving distance from Pismo Beach to Santa Cruz is 195 mi (315 km) and takes about 4.5 h. With lots of picture stops and perhaps a short hike and beach walk, you will need at least 8 hours for this part of the road trip.

Our first stop is **Morro Bay** where the main attraction is a big, round rock at one end of the bay. Scan the water close to the rock, especially if there is kelp on the surface. That's a favorite hiding spot of the **sea otters** from this area.

We continue to the next wildlife spotting place, **Elephant Seal** Viewing Point. Those colossi with their floppy nose are entertaining to watch since often, fights between males break out or the mothers are nursing their pups. We continue to the most impressive stretch of Highway 1; the part that leads through the area called **Big Sur**. In Big Sur, you will be gawking at many amazing, natural bay views. Don't forget to pull over! The must-do stop is at **McWay Falls** which drop onto the beach in a very picturesque bay. You can see the falls from the roadside viewing area. However, if you think it's time to stretch your legs, drive into the parking lot of Julia Pfeiffer Burns State Park. The state park is free with the *America the Beautiful* pass, otherwise, it costs $10. You can walk down to the falls on a short, 0.5 mi (800m)

hike (you won't come down to the beach since accessing the beach is forbidden). It's still a picturesque path worth taking. In case you are now encouraged to walk more, you have the choice to visit some other waterfalls in the forest.

Continue the stunning drive. About 20 miles before Monterrey, you will drive across another highlight along Highway 1; **Bixby Bridge**. Don't just drive across the beautiful bridge but stop at the viewpoint to take a picture or at least marvel at this impressive structure. Then, you reach **Monterrey**. This charming beach town would also be a good place to spend the night in case you think you've traveled far enough for today. Have a meal at the colorful **Old Fisherman's Wharf** and go **wildlife spotting** at the Coast Guard Pier. You might see sea lions and otters.

If you already want to get closer to San Francisco to have more time in that city, continue to **Santa Cruz** today (42 mi/ 67 km). It feels a bit similar to Santa Monica with a beautiful **boardwalk with rides**. Be sure to stop at **Capitola Beach** during daylight because there you find a very instagramable stretch of colorful houses.

Half Moon Bay – San Francisco

Today, we start the last part of our road trip along the Pacific Coast Highway. You cover a distance of 122 mi / 200 km, which takes about 2.5 hours if you don't stop anywhere. However, you should take a break at **Half Moon Bay**. The cliffs with the golden beach look very lovely and it's nice to spend time at such a natural beach again before heading into the vibrant city of **San Francisco**. More about SF you can read in the next chapter.

Highway 1 would lead another 170 miles (275 km) north to **Mendocino** (about 4h) but we leave the coast in San Francisco and drive via Oakland to Yosemite. This is quite a big detour away from the coast but the national park with the impressive mountains is worth it. After Yosemite, you should drive back to the coast via Sacramento toward **Eureka**. About 50 minutes before Eureka, there is a stretch of road you shouldn't miss; the **Avenue of the Giants**. It's a stunning drive below tall redwood trees. The whole drive between Yosemite and Eureka takes 8.5 hours. So, maybe you could even start driving toward Sacramento on the day you visit Yosemite.

San Francisco

In this city, you can marvel at the most photographed bridge in the world, ride historical trams, and enjoy sunny days in the beautiful bay area with various picturesque gardens. Well – if the sun isn't currently hiding behind a thick and freezing fog. In summer, often chilly air from the ocean rushes in to push away the heat which then results in a cold fog. Hence, be sure to always carry a light jacket with you when you're exploring SF. Otherwise, go hiding in one of the food halls or in a restaurant or shop in San Francisco's famous China Town.

How to get from the airport to the city center

SFO airport is located about 20 km outside the city center. You can drive into the city in about 25 minutes if you have a rental car. A taxi would cost about $55.
Otherwise, you can take bus 292 or 398 which brings you downtown in 1h 15 minutes for about $2.50.
A quicker way is by Bay Area Rapid Transit (BART) Metro. The trains leave about every 18 minutes and bring you downtown in 30 minutes for $9.65.
SF has a great public transport network, and you don't really need a car to visit the tourist sights.

The best things to do in San Francisco

Be it history, food, or nature, there are various things to do in the comparably small city of San Francisco.

Cross the Golden Gate Bridge

The stunning red bridge that shines in an even brighter color during sunset spans across the bay for 1.7 mi (2.7 km). This bridge is one of the sights you surely can't and don't want to ignore while being in San Francisco and you should have a look at it from different angles throughout the city. You can cross it by car, bicycle, or on foot. It's a great idea to rent a bike and enjoy the complete waterfront area between Fisherman's Warf and the Golden Gate Viewpoint across the bridge (5.9 mi/ 9.5 km – one way). In case you prefer a slower pace, you could take bus 130 from Union Square across the bridge and then walk back as far as you like. It's really nice to take a break and relax at the beach or Presidio Park. Be sure to stop by at the **Palace of Fine Arts** which is a beautiful building, surrounded by a lake.

Ride up and down the steep, winding streets

Have you seen a picture of a hairpin street with pretty flowers along the turns, surrounded by picturesque houses? That's San Francisco's iconic **Lombard Street**. Either drive down or train your leg muscles and walk it up or down but be sure to take a picture from the bottom looking up.
Just by driving around SF, you will see many other steep streets where you wonder whether your car will even make it up there, however, none of them are as curvy as Lombard Street. Since it's better to travel by public transport in order not to cause a traffic jam, you could take the opportunity and take one of SF's famous cable cars. **Hyde Street cable car** has a stop at the top of Lombard

Street and the **Powell-Mason cable car** has a stop at Lombard Street and Columbus Avenue. Either sit down and listen to the cable car's bell or stay standing and hang on to one of the hand-holders. One ride costs $8 no matter the distance and you need exact change, a *ClipperCard* or the *Muni mobile app*.

You can catch a bus to your next point of interest or even walk since most sights in SF aren't far from each other. A single-ride fare is $2.5 (mobile payment or transport card) or $3 (cash) and is valid for 2h.

Stroll past the most picturesque Victorian houses and be brought back to the flower power era

There still is a strong connection between San Francisco and peace, love, and happiness from the hippie movement. It's most palpable along **Haight** and **Ashbury** streets where you can look at colorful houses and lovely vintage shops. Be sure to also head to nearby Alamo Square, where the **Painted Ladies** are located, San Francisco's most iconic Victorian residential houses.

Relax at Golden Gate Park

This beautiful park offers lakes, playgrounds, a pasture with bison, green spaces, and flower gardens. After our road trip along the West Coast, we really enjoyed simply lazing around in the shade of the trees for half a day without doing much else.

Picturesque attractions inside the park are the **Japanese Gardens** with a tea house and the **Botanical Gardens**. Both cost $9 to enter. However, the Japanese Gardens can be entered for free before 10 a.m. on Monday, Wednesday, and Friday. Supposedly, this is where the first fortune cookies in the world were being served.

The Botanical Garden is pretty as well and free for SF-residents or free for everyone daily before 9 a.m. or on the second Tuesday of every month.

Eat seafood and spot sea lions at Fisherman's Wharf

At pier 39 you can indulge yourself in various seafood delicacies. Be careful though, that it doesn't accidentally get stolen by a seagull. Some more welcomed animal visitors are the sea lions that have chosen the docks at pier 39 as their home and are a beloved visitors' attraction. This whole area feels like a constant summer festival, and you can have a wonderful time along the water. A short walk from the pier you have the choice of many more touristy attractions like the Museum of 3D Illusions, Madame Tussauds, the Cartoon Art Museum, or Ripley's Believe it or Not! Hence, you could spend a full day in this area alone.

Travel to a different world in China Town

Enter China Town at **Dragon's Gate** and you will find yourself among red lanterns, shops with curious items, and delicious smells that come out of the restaurants.

This is one of the most famous Chinese communities outside of China.

Enjoy a meal at the Ferry Building

Next to Pier 1 you find the Ferry Building which is now a food market with market stalls that serve you lots of different delicacies. On Tuesdays, Thursdays, and Saturdays the outdoor space around the building turns into a farmer's market with fresh goods.

Take a tour of Alcatraz

Somehow, visiting a former prison doesn't seem appealing to me and therefore, I haven't actually done this tour. However, it seems to attract millions of other tourists each year and is one of the trips in San Francisco where you should purchase your ticket in advance: www.cityexperiences.com/san-francisco/city-cruises/alcatraz/tour-options/alcatraz-day-tour/

The tour price for an adult costs $41. You have to be at **Pier 33** a little bit before your ferry time. Then, you board the ferry which brings you across the bay to the island in about 15 minutes. You can explore the island on your own and will walk through the **prison on a self-guided audio tour**. When you are ready to return, head to the dock and catch the next ferry. Plan 2.5 to 3 hours for the tour and round trip.

Yosemite National Park

The drive from San Francisco to Yosemite takes about 3.5 hours (Big Oak Flat entrance) and it's not really on our path to the next sights. However, the vistas you have at Yosemite are so spectacular, that it's worth a detour. The scenery up here is much greener than in the national parks of the Southwest. You will see tall waterfalls and the famous **Half Dome** Mountain.

If you don't feel like driving yourself, you could take an organized day trip from SF. You can even reach it by train and bus but then you will have to spend a night in the Yosemite area before heading back. However, it's possible to visit the sights inside the national park without a car, since there is a free shuttle bus that brings visitors to 20 stops.

At the moment, you need to have a temporary reservation if you arrive as a private group. The reservation costs $2 (www.nps.gov/yose/planyourvisit/reservations.htm). The annual national park pass is valid at Yosemite. Without the park pass, the entry fee is $35 per vehicle.

The top things to do at Yosemite

Simply by driving through the park, you will be able to marvel at the top attractions like Tunnel View, Glacier Point, Yosemite Falls, and Half Dome.
The best time to visit Yosemite is spring when the waterfalls carry the most water. Fall is also beautiful when the leaves turn orange.

Take the most scenic drives

To see the most popular sights, drive the **Yosemite Valley Loop**. You can enjoy the sights of El Capitan, Half Dome, Bridalveil Falls, and Yosemite Falls. You can stop along the way to do a shorter or longer hike. Best let yourself be guided by the beauty of nature and simply head in the direction that attracts you most.
Glacier Point Road will take you to a higher elevation and in the end, you will be rewarded with the incredible view from **Glacier Point**.

Hikes at Yosemite

You could fill more than a week with hiking inside Yosemite. Therefore, it's best if you either just wing it with some short hikes that you find while driving through the park or you look around on the national park's website and pick out the ones that attract you most: www.nps.gov/yose/planyourvisit/valleyhikes.htm

The most famous hike at Yosemite is getting on top of the **Half Dome**. It is a tough and also slightly dangerous hike. Hence, it will need some training and preparation and you can't just arrive at Yosemite and attempt the hike. Plus, you need an extra hiking permission which has nothing to do with the general park entry permission. Check this website to read how it works with spending the night at Yosemite or obtaining a hiking permission for the Half Dome: www.nps.gov/yose/planyourvisit/hdpermits.htm.

Watch the climbers

Finally, Yosemite is famous for rock climbing and many records in free climbing. Scan the huge, gray walls in the park and you will surely spot some brave climbers. Frequent Yosemite visitors even arrive with camping chairs which they set up in good spots to watch the spectacle.

Once you took some deep breaths of the clean air out here and are satisfied with the beauty of nature that you have witnessed, you should start your drive toward Sacramento, in order to continue your road trip.

Red Wood drive-through trees and distance to Seattle

From Sacramento, you could save a lot of time by just following the I-5 north to Portland. However, you are here to see some spectacular sights, right? Therefore, put **Chandelier Tree** as the next destination on your map. It's one of three remaining drive-through trees. Each tree costs $5 to $10 to drive through and perhaps one experience will be enough for you. Either way, it's an impressive sight when a tree trunk is so broad that a whole car can fit through it. **Shrine Tree** is just a short drive away.

Halfway between there and Eureka you are in for another treat. An about 30 miles long (48 km) part of the drive will lead you through especially tall redwood trees. You might feel as if you are driving in a natural tunnel. This is called **Avenue of the Giants** and is named one of the most beautiful drives along the West Coast.

With **Eureka,** you have made it back to the ocean. This is a lovely place to spend the night since, apart from the beach, there also are many charming, castle-like houses.

In case you wondered about the third drive-through tree, it's called **Klamath Tour Through Tree** and is situated directly along Highway 101 which you take anyway while proceeding toward Portland.

The drive from Eureka to **Portland** is another long day on which you cover 410 miles (660 km). The drive will take you about 7h. Now, you have reached the green state of Oregon. However, we won't stay long since we're only a short way from the end of our amazing road trip. **Seattle** in the state of Washington lies just another 3h (175 mi / 280 km) north.

Portland

The state of Oregon is still a well-kept travel secret since it receives fewer visitors than California. However, when you reach Portland on your road trip you will surely already have been impressed by the stunning coastal views or the blue lakes in **Crater Lake National Park**. In the city of Portland, you can enjoy picturesque gardens, great street food, or craft coffee and beer.

From the airport to the city center

PDX airport has repeatedly been voted as the best US airport. Its advantages are a good working WIFI, nice shopping facilities, and dining options as well as a very convenient connection to the city center.
You can take the red metro line (MAX light rail) which brings you downtown in 35 minutes for $2.50. It runs from 4.45.a.m. until 11.50 p.m.

The best things to do in Portland – a one-day itinerary

Start your day at a **charming or hip café** with the special house blend. If it's a Saturday, you should then head to **Saturday Market**.

In any case, you then take a **stroll along Willamette River** on the **Waterfront Park Trail**. Continue to the lively **Pioneer Courthouse Square** in the downtown area, where always something is going on. Then, simply wander around Portland's city center and see what you discover along the way. Once you are hungry, head to **5th Avenue Food Cart Pod**. It's a constant outdoor food truck market where you can enjoy flavors from around the world.

With a full belly, you take the Red or Blue line MAX tram to the Oregon Zoo stop at Washington Park. Our next goal is the very picturesque **International Rose Test Garden**. It's free to enter and once at Washington Park, you could walk there or take a free *Explore Washington Park shuttle*.

Another that would be worth a visit is the **Lan Su Chinese Garden** which is near Saturday Market and offers a tranquil oasis in the city center in an exotic setting. However, it costs $10 for adults to enter. Or the **Japanese Garden** where you can enjoy many pretty ponds. It's also located at Washington Park, however; it costs $16.95 to enter! Hence, with all the other beautiful, free parks in Portland, you should only visit the Japanese Gardens if you want a temporary escape to Japan.

Have dinner at a pub with **local craft beer** and sample assorted flavors.
In case you are in Portland while the weather isn't so good, a great alternative to walks in the parks would be to **join a brewery tour** and sample some beer. Over seventy breweries are located in Portland, and you surely find a tour that you'd enjoy. Just bear in mind that you need to be older than twenty-one to drink alcohol.

Seattle

Whether you know the Space Needle out of Grey's Anatomy or you want to come here because it's known for its coffee culture and the first Starbucks in the world, Seattle has many surprises in store for you and is a city that shouldn't be overlooked on the tourist trail.

From the airport to the city center

SEA airport is located about 20 minutes by car from the city center. Uber and Lyft are available, and a taxi would cost between $40 and $55.
A much cheaper and also very convenient option is the **Link light rail**. Trains run every 8 to 15 minutes and the fare will be between $2.25 and $3.50, depending on how far you go. The journey downtown takes about 35 minutes.

You can also purchase an ORCA transport card for $5 and charge it with a day-pass for $8. With the day-pass, you can also use the cool *Seattle Center Monorail* between Westlake Center downtown and the base of Queen Anne hill, on which one ride normally costs $3.

The best things to do in Seattle

In Seattle, you can visit one of the most awesome markets in the US, one of the best museums in the world, and enjoy tranquil nature as well.

Visit one of the coolest museums in the world

First of all, the EMP Museum of Pop Culture (MoPOP) is an architectural masterpiece that you have to take a look at from the outside. Secondly, it's an interactive and entertaining museum where you learn about music history and artists. I really enjoyed my visit and would go back any time. You should buy your ticket online (www.empmuseum.org/) where you sometimes can save money if you take a time slot with less visitors. However, expect to pay between $25 and $28. The museum is closed on Wednesday.

Enjoy the view from the Space Needle

The iconic Space Needle was opened in 1962 for the World Fair. It should appear like a flying saucer. The height is 605 feet (185 m) and there are three viewing areas: an indoor observation deck and an open-air viewing terrace on the second level and a new, revolving glass floor 360° observation deck on the first level. You can ride up to the observation decks by elevator in 43 seconds and enjoy the view during daylight or night hours.

General admission is $35 but you can buy a ticket with a day and evening admission for $59.

Another attraction at the bottom of the Space Needle is the **Chihuly Garden and Glass** exhibition. This North American artist is famous for blowing beautiful flower constructions out of glass and his art is present around the world. Admission to his glasshouse is $32 but you can buy a combined ticket with the Space Needle for $57 (https://sn.web.ticketing.siaticketing.com/).

Explore the sights and the food at Pike Place Market

Pike Place Market is more than just a food market hall. While you find many restaurants and eateries, there are also street buskers, retail shops, arts and crafts shops, and a farmer's market.

Another highlight at Pike Place Market is *The Gum Wall*. You find it like this on Google Maps. It has turned into a permanent art installation where people can stick their chewing gum to a wall that is already covered in gum. It's there to make aware of all the gum that might otherwise be thrown to the ground carelessly and harm the environment.

Plus, a fun fact, the Starbucks that you see at Pike Place Market is the first one that has ever been opened. Therefore, the line here is much longer than at other Starbucks, although the interior is no different than how we know our beloved sweet coffee brewer from around the world. If you like the smell of coffee, you should pilgrim to the Starbucks Roastery nine blocks from Pike Place Market (1124 Pike St), where you can book tours or try new blends at the café.

Watch salmon migrate and boats being lifted

Seattle has a cool water channel area called the **Ballard Locks**. It was constructed so that boats could pass between Puget Sound and Lake Union. The boats have to wait in a water lift, where either water is being let out or let in, in order to even out the water level of Puget Sound and Lake Union. Once the water is even, the boat can continue its journey. This spectacle is free to visit and attracts many curious visitors who want to enjoy some sunshine along the water.

A cool side effect is that salmon can also use this area to migrate. There is a free visitor center with underwater windows, where you can watch how the fish jump or swim from one chamber into the next. You might see Sockeye, Chinook, or Coho salmon.

Check Google Maps for your best bus connection from the city (the drive takes about 25 minutes with 8 minutes of walking, $2.75).

Next to Ballard Locks is *Carl S. English Jr. Botanical Garden* which is also a nice spot to hang out and enjoy sunrays.

Stroll through the Olympic Sculpture Park

This free park belongs to the Seattle Museum of Art. It's a nice green space in the waterfront area where you can marvel at sculptures while enjoying a leisurely stroll.

Border Crossing into Canada: Seattle to Vancouver

When you are in Seattle, you are only 143 mi (231 km) from one of Canada's most famous cities; Vancouver. Without any additional COVID regulations (check before you travel), it's just a simple bus, train, or car ride from Seattle to Vancouver, as long as your passport is valid.

Traveling by bus is the cheapest option. Prices range from $1 (!) to $40 for one way, so compare the different companies like Greyhound, QuickBus, or Bolt Bus online. The journey takes around 4 hours.

The train ride with Amtrak is a bit faster and incredibly scenic. Prices start at $45.

What to do in Vancouver

Vancouver is famous for having a beautiful yacht harbor and ocean front while being surrounded by several world class ski resorts. One way to experience the beauty of both is to drive the **Sea-to-Sky Highway** which brings you from downtown Vancouver to Whistler Mountain in 1.5 hours with many scenic attractions along the way.

If you don't want to leave the water, rent a bicycle and ride around picturesque **Stanley Park** (or go for a walk but you will see more by bicycle).

For a cool hike, head to Lynn Canyon (https://lynncanyon.ca/) where you can enjoy pretty walks in the forest and cross a thrilling suspension bridge.

My Couchsurfing host convinced me that I have to try a **Japadog**, which is a hot dog but mixed with Japanese ingredients. It was very delicious, and you shouldn't let the opportunity pass to try this special food that I've only found in Vancouver so far.

Finally, go out or go shopping in the **Gastown** district which is similar to San Diego's Gaslamp quarter, and it would be a nice ending to the trip by kind of coming full circle this way.

About the author of this guidebook

Seraina loves to travel since she can remember.
It started with beach vacations with her family when she was a child but soon, she sought her own routes. She was lucky to be able to spend an amazing High School year in New York at 15 years old. That's when she started to write her first travel blog which evolved into *SwissMissOnTour*. Then, she also visited California for the first time and enjoyed a road trip through the national parks with her family.
Later, she explored Europe with Interrail but was also attracted by the exotic countries further away. Countless trips to Southeast Asia made her fall in love with the delicious Asian flavors, beautiful temples, and nature highlights.
On a trip around the world, she spent a lot of time in Australia and New Zealand, re-visiting the US on her way back to Switzerland.
During shorter vacations, Central America with its picturesque beaches often called out to her.
Her last big adventure led Swissmissontour to South America and of course back to the USA.

Unfortunately, the coronavirus pandemic has forced her to return to Switzerland earlier than intended. Since then, she has explored more of Switzerland and pretty much any country nearby that opened its borders :P
Now, a new adventure is in store for her, as she is expecting her first baby. Traveling will surely be different with a small child but count on it that you will read more good travel tips from Swissmissontour.

Do you need more info?

In case you need more info, I am happy to help. Contact or follow me through these channels. Especially on Instagram you can enjoy daily travel tips, inspiration, and travel quotes.

(b) www.swissmissontour.com

(i) @swissmissontour

(f) SwissMissOnTour

(w) www.slgigerbooks.wordpress.com

Did you like this travel guide?

In case you liked this travel guide, I'd greatly appreciate a positive review on Amazon, and it would be a good support if you told your friends about it 😊

More books by S. L. Giger

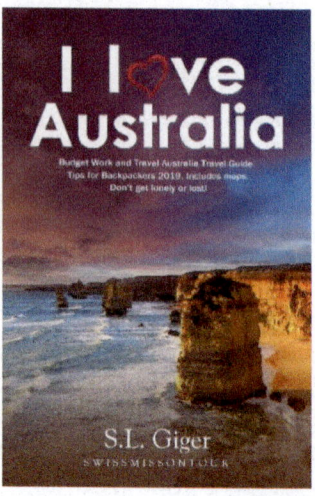

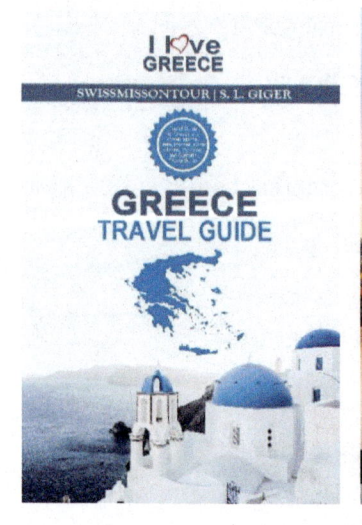

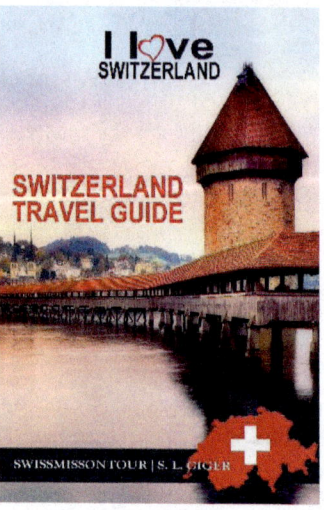

Printed in Great Britain
by Amazon